Embodying Ecological Heritage
in a Maya Community

Embodying Ecological Heritage in a Maya Community

Health, Happiness, and Identity

Kristina Baines

LEXINGTON BOOKS
Lanham • Boulder • New York • London

Published by Lexington Books
An imprint of The Rowman & Littlefield Publishing Group, Inc.
4501 Forbes Boulevard, Suite 200, Lanham, Maryland 20706
www.rowman.com

Unit A, Whitacre Mews, 26-34 Stannary Street, London SE11 4AB

British Library Cataloguing in Publication Information Available

Library of Congress Cataloging-in-Publication Data

Names: Baines, Kristina, 1973–
Title: Embodying ecological heritage in a Maya community : health, happiness, and identity / Kristina Baines.
Description: Lanham : Lexington Books, 2016. | Includes bibliographical references.
Identifiers: LCCN 2015036104| ISBN 9781498512824 (hardcover : alkaline paper) | ISBN 9781498512831 (ebook) | ISBN 9781498512848 (pbk : alkaline paper)
Subjects: LCSH: Mayas—Belize—Social life and customs. | Mayas—Belize—Social conditions. | Ethnology—Belize. | Human ecology—Belize. | Community life—Belize. | Environmental health—Belize. | Health services accessibility—Belize. | Land tenure—Belize. | Education—Social aspects—Belize. | Belize—Ethnic relations.
Classification: LCC F1435.3.S7 B35 2016 | DDC 305.80097282—dc23
LC record available at http://lccn.loc.gov/2015036104

♾™ The paper used in this publication meets the minimum requirements of American
National Standard for Information Sciences Permanence of Paper for Printed Library
Materials, ANSI/NISO Z39.48-1992.

Printed in the United States of America

This book is dedicated to the memory of two grandmothers who, through struggles I will never have to endure, taught me the skills to embody my ecological heritage.

Linda Pansy Cooper Baines

(2 February 1919–8 May 2008)

and

Florentina "Ixna Lola" Coc

(22 October 1940–26 August 2013)

Contents

Acknowledgments

I am very fortunate and grateful to have received so much encouragement and support from many people during the researching and writing of this book. I would first like to thank the people of the Toledo District, Belize, especially the members of the community of Santa Cruz. Their endless enthusiasm, patience and willingness to assist in so many ways were, and continue to be, invaluable to me. It is an important and changing time in southern Belize, and I am especially inspired by the way in which I was invited and trusted to witness the negotiation of changes in the community in real time. Without people welcoming me into their homes, sharing *wah* and *caldo* and teaching me to bake, I would never have been able to begin to understand this negotiation and tell this story. I am fortunate to have been able to learn from so many people in Santa Cruz and around Belize, many of whom are named in this book and many more to whom I hope I have personally expressed my gratitude. I cannot say it enough and I hope this book will honor the time and effort you gave so that your important story could be told. *B'otik tech!*

I am grateful for the ongoing support of my advisors and colleagues during the research and writing process. Foremost, I am grateful for the multi-faceted support of Becky K. Zarger. Without her, I likely would never have come to know Belize in the way that I have had the privilege of knowing it. I am grateful for the advice of Keith Prufer and the understanding of Doug Reeser. I have great appreciation for Amy Thompson, who was integral in thinking through and preparing the final drafts of the book. For their ongoing interest and support through the research process, I am grateful to Bruce Winterhalder, Heide Casteñeda, Daniel Lende, and Fenda Akiwumi. Most recently, Molly Makris has kept me smiling and moving forward—thank you!

I am also grateful for the financial support of the National Science Foundation, Human Social Dynamics Program and the University of South Florida Department of Anthropology, which funded the research for my doctoral dissertation, which would become this book. I would also like to express my gratitude to Nigel Encalada and the team at the Institute of Social and Cultural Research and National Institute of Culture and History in Belize for their encouragement of this project and other important social and cultural research in Belize.

I would also like to give special thanks for the interest, support and tenacity of the editorial staff at Lexington Books, especially Amy King and Francinia Williams.

A final, and deeply felt, expression of thanks goes to my friends and family. Thank you all for your conviction that I would indeed complete this research and book, and for your listening to my stories and struggles, through varying degrees of interest. Cooper Myers—your positivity and willingness try new things is an inspiration to me in Belize and every-where. It is difficult to thank you enough for understanding the work your mother does and supporting both when you are by my side and when we are far away from each other. Victoria Costa—your incredible support in every realm is deeply woven into this book. At every stage of the research process and writing process, your intellectual, emotional, and practical partnership made this possible. I am ridiculously fortunate to share this, and every, journey with you. For true.

ONE

Beginning at the End:
"He Is Nearly Dead"

It was already dark as I came up over the hill at the entrance to the village. Normally, the darkness is punctuated only by the occasional glimpse of a candle or gas lamp flickering through gaps in the wooden plank walls of the houses. This evening, the house in my line of sight as I slowly moved the truck down the rocky road was brightly lit. Light shone through cotton dresses, highlighting the purposeful movements of the ladies. Children and young men stood and wandered on the grassy slope outside the open door. As I approached, a friend came down the slope to the open window of the truck.

"Kristina. He is nearly dead."

"Your uncle?"

"Yes. You are coming?"

"Yes."

As I slowly pulled off the road and stopped on the grassy verge in front of the house, my passenger quickly slipped out and walked up the slope with the other young men who had come to greet him. I had picked him up by chance in San Antonio, a nearby village. In the four miles of slow road in between the villages, I came to learn that he had been sent for. He had been called to Santa Cruz because his father was dying. I knew he was not from the village because of my acquaintance with everybody residing there, but, had I not; his soft, rounded face would have given me a strong clue. Santa Cruz's young men his age—around 20 years—were noticeably different, faces leaner with weather and work. He had grown up in a village further north, close to the Southern highway where it was now unusual for young men his age to build and thatch houses and plant corn.

"My father has diabetes. That is his sickness."

1

"How do you know?"

"The doctor said. He used to be very fat and now he is thin."

"Why do you think he has it?"

"When he started to work on the buses, he started to drink many Coca-Colas every day. I tell him to drink water but he doesn't want to listen."

His demeanor was reserved and polite but he spoke freely and plainly. I did not detect anger or panic. When we arrived at the illuminated house where his father lay, he took his place among his cousins and we didn't speak again. I was ushered up the grassy slope and into the dimly lit thatch adjacent to the main house, which housed the *k'ob'en* or fire hearth, and given a tamale of steamed ground corn and chicken wrapped in a *le'che* or waha leaf. The ladies filled me in on the latest developments with their uncle. Over the past several days, he had stopped speaking. He had stopped standing up on his own. He did not want to eat anything. These events were an indication that death was coming and tonight the family had called an emergency service to focus on prayer and ask for his life. They had brought the generator from the Baptist church to supply power for the light and the electric keyboard used to accompany the hymns. They would be here all night praying and feeding those who came to pray with them.

In the main house, wooden pews carried from the church filled up all available space with the exception of two hammocks strung across the center of the room. In one hammock, the sick man lay sprawled on his side, his faced pressed into the woven cotton cord. His skin was loose and pale. In the next hammock, sitting upright and facing him, was his mother, her silver hair and dark skin glowing despite the palpable worry in her face for her son. Under the first hammock stood a half-full plastic bottle of Coca-Cola. The pews were filled with Baptist worshippers, mostly extended family of the man, singing, clapping, and praying in unison and, at times, whenever the spirit struck them. Groups of close family were moved to kneel on the cement floor close to the hammock, directing their prayer. The sick man, with assistance, was encouraged to raise and offer his prayers aloud. He did this several times over the course of the night.

The sick man did not die. There were small improvements over the next days and weeks and, eventually, he felt well enough to leave his mother's house in Santa Cruz and go back to the village by the highway where he had been living. Reports about his health in the months that followed were scattered and mixed. He was working on the bus again. He had been given another prayer service in the other village. He had disappeared and his wife did not know where he was. He had gained weight but then was thin again. I still ask when I visit with his family but answers are not definitive.

I begin with this vignette neither to offer a simple indictment of multinational soft drink corporations nor to provide an affirmation of the efficacy of prayer, but as an illustration of how practices and perceptions of illness and wellness in the Belizean Mopan Maya community of Santa Cruz are explicitly woven together with thoughts about work, place, family and food and the choices that people make surrounding these ideas and practices. In some cases, this weaving together is tight and clear, but, as in the case of this opening illustration, most of the connections are nuanced and malleable. In writing this ethnography, I aim to clarify the connections between health and wellness and these aspects of daily life that might be termed "traditional" ecological knowledge (TEK) and practice. These connections are significant in that they allow for a more complete understanding of how wellness is defined and maintained in Santa Cruz, as well as providing a tangible measure, in the form of the body, of the importance of engaging with TEK and practice. Both the defining and maintaining of health and wellness, and TEK, and its relationship to heritage, are domains of anthropological interest, both theoretically and practically. I argue, through the data and discussion presented here, for an explicit consideration of the interdependence of wellness and traditional ecological practice and propose the term "embodied ecological heritage" to describe and theorize this interdependence. Healthy bodies are defined and maintained through this heritage practice and the data in the following chapters demonstrate how.

I first came to Santa Cruz in May of 2009 with an interest in both health/wellness and environmental knowledge/practice. Taken on as part of an interdisciplinary team of a National Science Foundation grant funded project[1] and tasked with collaboratively designing and teaching environmental and cultural heritage research to the community's children, I was afforded an ideal ethnographic opportunity to become familiar with the 76 families and acres of lowland forests that are Santa Cruz. My popularity with the children and passable tortilla-making skills, coupled with the open generosity of so many of the residents, made for easy conversation. It was during one of these conversations that the trajectory for this research came into focus. During the summer of 2010, over the course of a couple of weeks, several of the ladies had expressed concern about a neighbor and mother of ten who had been suffering beatings from her husband. The lady, they reported and I later confirmed, did not want help. The *alcalde*, or village law enforcement leader, had been informed. Putting aside my initial anger and frustration, what struck me was that the ladies who spoke to me about the incident did not focus on the physical scars and emotional trauma of the mother subjected to the abuse. They focused on what they viewed as a more important way in which her husband had hurt her: he had not made a farm that planting cycle. He had not planted his corn. One of my closest allies looked at me in earnest and said, "Kristina, good men grow corn." This statement is

one of many illustrations of how traditional practices, in this case, argu-
ably, the most important traditional Maya practice, growing corn, are
linked to broad definitions of being well. "Good," in this sense, means
necessary for a "good life," which includes being healthy and happy.
Additionally, it could have been said that "good women process and
prepare corn," indicating that women's work, as the following chapters
show, is just as important to health as men's work. The men in Santa
Cruz would easily confirm this as truth if the data are deemed inconclusive.

Having spent two consecutive summers in Santa Cruz turning research findings into lessons and teaching these to eager students, my
research questions solidified and I began to consider ways in which to
investigate the health/environmental knowledge and practice intersection. I wanted to understand how health and wellness were conceived in
the community and if and how they were related to ecological practice
and experience. Also, I wondered how environmental heritage was conceived of and manifested in an individual and in a community, and if this
concept was even salient or related to environmental knowledge and skill
or wellness, broadly conceived to include ideas of happiness. Finally, I
sought to understand if environmental knowledge and skill were related
to the way the body is conceptualized and how this might intersect with
what I found about wellness.

When I returned to Santa Cruz in April of 2011 to stay for the remainder of the year, I had already amassed a wealth of ethnographic data and
was looking to qualify and quantify what I had found. In order to clarify
the wellness and TEK relationship, my objective was to gain a clear picture of each, immersing myself in the rhythms of daily life while collecting data related to health and important ecological practices: informal
wellness interviews (n = 45), free lists (n = 50), one unconstrained pile sort
(n = 24) and two constrained pile sorts (n = 30 each), an environmental
heritage and wellness assessment survey (n = 64), time-allocation spot
observations, formal interviews (n = 20), and a consensus survey (n = 12).
These daily lives I was privileged to participate in were shaped by a
particular social and ecological history of which I was aware, both
through study and conversation, but also because of what I did with my
body.

BEING WELL, BEING MAYA

My experiences living and collecting data in Santa Cruz allowed me to
explore a framework, which I refer to as "embodied ecological heritage."
This served as both a guide and a lens through which to make sense of
both the data and my everyday life. It grew in response to the lack of
ways to consider and explain how a healthy body (and mind) and tradi-

tional ecological knowledge and practice might be related, both in scholarly and popular discourse, beyond ethnobotanical linkages. It allows the discussion to move toward a more detailed understanding of how bodies change through ecological interactions. These broader links are just beginning to be explored through detailed ethnographic example. Embodied ecological heritage provides a framework to think about what these examples show.

Each of the constituent terms of "embodied ecological heritage" carries with it a set of conceptions, which add value to the framework. In Baines (forthcoming), each of the constituent terms is fully unpacked and set alongside alternate perspectives to illustrate their utility. Below is a brief explanation of how these terms come together to serve as the guiding theoretical framework for this data and discussion.

Embodied

Health and wellness are theorized, observed, and measured using a wide range of perspectives and instruments. In this study, I define health and wellness broadly, assessing both "people's own internal states of mind" as well as conducting "external observation and evaluation" (Mathews and Izquierdo 2009) to include: individual perceptions; social context; and physical behavior and bodily manifestations related to community-generated, contextualized definitions of health, wellness, well-being, and happiness, while rejecting Cartesian assumptions separating physical and mental health. This holistic definition is echoed in the current definition of health provided by the World Health Organization (WHO), which explicitly includes these components.

A focus on the individual body, and the effects of daily sensory experiences and practice on the body, lends itself to a phenomenological perspective, in the Heideggerian philosophical tradition. The term "embodied" and its reference to embodiment reflects this phenomenological root and considers how it was taken up by medical anthropologists considering holistic effects of experience on the body (Csordas 1994; Holmes 2013). A focus on embodied experience allows for mind/body dualisms to collapse through shifting the focus from distinction between what is thought and practiced to what is experienced as a whole. I argue that this focus on the "whole experience" goes far to facilitate a collapse of the health/wellness/happiness distinctions and considering the embodied experience (and embodying the experience myself). My choice of the term "embodied" reflects an effort to collapse the distinctions and I reject the assumption that "health" is an objective, physical measure while "wellness" is subjective, associated with the development of biomedical models of health (Good 1993). The use of a phenomenological perspective in guiding this study does not fundamentally reject its awareness of, or contributions to, other perspectives or theoretical streams within medical anthropology. External socio-political factors are considered as they are reflected in the lived experience of individuals. Although individuals embody their own wellness experience, the many social and environmental forces guide the nature of this embodiment. In many cultures and communities, including Santa Cruz, personal autonomy is valued but it is "not independence but an autonomy that is continuously constituted *within* the social" (Heil 2009: 108). The social, then, along with the environmental, must be considered in this discussion. While phenomenological in focus, the study does make contributions to a more politically focused Critical Medical Anthropology (Baer et al. 2003) and a socially focused "biocultural synthesis" (Leatherman, Goodman, and Thomas 1993). These contributions are discussed further in the concluding chapter.

Ecological

I use the term "ecological" in two ways, also highlighting the connections between these usages. Firstly, the term refers most simply to elements of the natural environment and their many linkages and interactions: land, plants, animals and seasonal weather cycles, as examples. In this sense, "ecological" is considered as an alternative to more explicitly social, political, or cognitively focused ways of describing and understanding human behavior. Secondly, the term is used to refer, more specifically, to the body of literature referring to and cataloguing TEK. In this usage, extracting the term "ecological" is meant to reflect a critique of the terms "traditional" and "knowledge" while referencing the scholarship related to TEK as informing this research and its theoretical framework.

I recognize the problematic nature of the term TEK, utilizing it with caution and defining it broadly. The following definition is recognized for these purposes: TEK [is] a term used to describe the knowledge held by indigenous cultures about their immediate environments and the cultural (management) practices that build on that knowledge" (Ford and Martinez 2000). Informants in this study used the terms "traditional" and "tradition" to broadly indicate practices and knowledge handed down from parents and grandparents and, in many cases, considered to be what "Maya people" have done or known for hundreds of years or longer.

There is a recent scholarly push for an incorporation of process-oriented studies, moving beyond descriptions of TEK in terms of what people know and how they talk about it, to understanding how the knowledge changes as part of an ongoing interconnected and interactive process through what they do. It is this process of interconnection and its explicit consideration that informs the frame for this research, particularly as it informs the construction of ecological heritage. Without a recognition and consideration of the dynamic nature of ecological knowledge and practice, this heritage is difficult to understand or measure. This study, in this sense, both relies on and demonstrates the fluidity of TEK.

Heritage

My use of the term "heritage" carries with it the dangers of leading down a theoretical rabbit hole, however; it is precisely the potentially problematic nature of the term that attracted me. The malleable and politicized nature of heritage definition contributes to its need for analysis and clarification: in this case, through the bodily experience of ecological practice. "Traditions" and "histories" begin to evoke what is meant by heritage, however, they fall short in both their failure to capture the dynamic nature of the construction of the past in the present. While these terms reference past events, "heritage" evokes the interaction with the past in the present. This is an important distinction in the development of the theoretical frame for the research and analyses presented here.

Because "heritage is an interpretation, adaptation, exploitation, or a creation in the present rather than a preservation of what actually exists" (Chan 2005: 66), traditional knowledge and practices plus the thoughts about the implications of "being Maya" all play a role in its construction. Rather than deny "the witting or unwitting role of anthropologists in the creation of heritage" (Olwig 1999: 370), I argue here that taking into account how multiple inputs, in the form of personal interactions, daily sensory experience, as well as more overt activist discussions, is what makes this type of constructed heritage useful. This creation process has a direct effect on a person's lived experience of, in this case, "being Maya." Thus, it becomes embodied heritage, fundamentality different from the kind of disembodied list of traditions or collections of knowledge that are critiqued previously. People can interact with heritage in multiple ways and, because it is both fluid and embodied, multiple "heritages" can exist not only in one community but also in one person. Rather than being problematic, the existence of multiple heritages necessitates and benefits from a phenomenological approach.

Ecological heritage might be considered a subset of cultural heritage. "Cultural heritage does not end at monuments and collections of objects. It also includes traditions or living expressions inherited from our ancestors and passed on to our descendants" (Blake 2002). It could be argued that each person holds a unique environmental heritage related to his/her own interactions with their natural world through his/her life. A discussion of environmental heritage requires a particular set of considerations, for example, the level of engagement an individual has with their natural environment or how that environment has changed over time. However, I argue that similar issues and definitions—those related to representation, authenticity and significance—are part of this discussion, just as they are when considering the preservation of an ancient building.

I find the distinct between tangible and intangible heritage (McKercher and du Cros 2002: 83) problematic and show through this ethnography that the lived experience makes that which might be called intangible tangible through the body. In the sense that children pick fruit from trees and men use sticks to make holes to plant corn, there is a strong tangible element to environmental heritage.

EMBODIED ECOLOGICAL HERITAGE: LAYING THE FOUNDATION

"The ecological body as heritage might be thought of as a way of getting at an intersection of the classic theoretical concepts of habitus and embodiment" (Baines 2011: 303; Baines forthcoming). Ecological "knowledge" and ecological "practice" are used in this discussion in conjunction and, in some cases, interchangeably. The conflation of knowledge and practice, I argue, is not problematic in a discussion of embodied ecological heritage, with all three constituent terms allowing for a discussion of both.

Lauer and Aswani (2009: 318) problematize the word "knowledge" and "its root in questionable epistemological assumptions of abstraction, formality and articulation." This critique is especially salient in many indigenous communities, including Belizean Maya communities, where learning more typically happens in situ, or in practice (Zarger 2002), as opposed to in this formal, knowledge-based way. Reports of knowledge in my research in Santa Cruz often took the form of "I remember it because we used to do it when I was young" rather than "I was taught it but don't do it." Abstract knowledge without foundation in practice, particularly knowledge related to tradition or heritage, was rarely observed or discussed.

Taken up and outlined most explicitly by Bourdieu (1977), habitus describes how bodily learning takes place, in a sense, without the conscious cognition typically understood to accompany the learning process. Embodied activity, Crossley (1996: 99) explains, "takes up these habitual schema and deploys them, in situ, with competence and skill." This is what this study has hoped to capture. Essentially, knowledge and practice come together through physical application. A consideration of environmental knowledge and practice in this frame allows for a more fluid understanding of both the biological and the social. The research presented here seeks to push beyond existing theoretical divides and, through an ethnographic study of human/environment interactions, further flesh out what is essentially a "cognitive phenomenology," something that, in the past, would likely have been described as an oxymoron.

There is some precedent for attempts at understanding intersections between changes in the body and the environment. Taking the generation of knowledge as an ongoing process in which individuals learn about their bodies (and, consequently, bodily health) in a "give and take" inter-action with their natural environment, Ingold (2000) incorporates ideas of sensory experience and cognitive patterning as reflections of a greater understanding of how individuals operate in the world. Using his "pro-cessing loop" model, the individual experiences of sensation, touch and taste, for example, are indicators provided by the natural environment as to the properties and effectiveness of a food, herb, or medicine. However, neither his or other models of body/ecology interactions (for example, Hsu's "body ecologic" [2007: 92]) explicitly outlines how ecological skill actually acts on biology or provides a clear mechanism for understanding how the wellness of an individual or a community is practically affected by the process of becoming enskilled through ecological knowledge. That is the approach taken here.

The following chapters address these lacunae through ethnographic detail and a variety of data collection methods and analyses. Figure 1.1 shows an example of how knowledge/practice and body/environment intersections might be understood in terms of an ecological processing loop based on the ethnographic example related earlier in this chapter. It shows how wellness can be defined broadly, in terms of mind and bodily health, and how environmental practice plays an important role in the process. This type of phenomenological processing loop will be used as a method of clarifying "embodied ecological heritage" throughout the fol-lowing chapters. The term "processing loop" is used here to describe and illustrate instances and experiences in which the wellness/ecology rela-tionship might be seen as circular. The figures presented are intended to illustrate the phenomenological discussion and are not intended to ex-plain causal relationships or more complex human/ecology interactions and evolutionary relationships. It is my hope that the illustration of these relationships and how they are woven together, through these loops and the wider ethnography, will remind us that practice, knowledge, and wellness are not linear concepts and revealing their connections and com-plexities is crucial to challenging assumptions that they are.

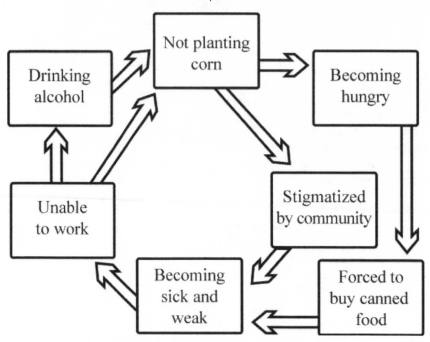

Figure 1.1 Phenomenological Processing Loop: Good Men Grow Corn

NOTE

1. "Development and Resilience of Complex Socioeconomic Systems: A Theoretical Model and Case Study from the Maya Lowlands." National Science Foundation, Human Social Dynamics Program Collaborative Grant (2008–2013). Grant award #0827281. Douglas Kennett (PI Oregon), Keith Prufer (Co-PI UNM), Rebecca Zarger, (Co-PI USF), Bruce Winterhalder (Co-PI UC-Davis).

TWO

The Mopan Maya in Belize: "They Do It Different Across"

"D'yoos," I called out as I climbed the small grassy hill and poked my head in the open door of the thatch house. I knew she would be inside, even though it was dark and, with eyes adjusted to the sunshine of my walk to reach there, I couldn't make out any of the shapes. I stood in the doorway looking in, behaving slightly more intrusively than I would have at most of the other homes in the village. She was one of my closest allies here and had hailed me this morning to wash our clothes together at the river. I had brought along my white, plastic five-gallon bucket and set it by the open door. It had once held lard, the preferred cooking fat here, but now held my dirty skirts and blouses. I peered into the darkness and saw the mud floor was swept clean and recently patched and smoothed, the rings of moisture from this process still evaporating in the growing heat of the day. I scanned the spacious single room that made up the house. Both tables were set against the wall, cups and dishes neatly stacked. The *k'ob'en* (firehearth) was straight ahead, emitting a fading glow as the last of the morning's firewood was left to extinguish itself without anyone tending to it. The wooden plank platform bed to my right was covered in a brightly colored woven blanket pulled neatly across its boards.

"Ok'en." Her voice came from the hammock in the center of the house and sounded weaker than was normal. At that invitation, I stepped across the threshold and walked toward where she was. She smiled up at me but, uncharacteristically, did not rise. It was clear to me she was in pain again.

"How are you?"

"I am okay. I will be okay."

"You are okay?"

11

"Kristina, I have pain in my belly again."

Pain, for her, was a common occurrence. The first summer I spent in Santa Cruz, I was invited to bake tortillas at her mother-in-law's home at the base of the small hill I'd just climbed—maybe 30 feet away. Many ladies were hailed to bake that day because their husbands and fathers were helping her husband to build the house I was now standing in. She had been married more than two years at that time and, while it is more customary to wait until children are born to a couple before leaving the husband's parents' house, they had made the decision to move without them. By the time I had passed my second summer in the village, she and I had grown close enough for her to share that the reason she believed that they had not had children was related to the pain she felt in her abdomen. There was a problem. She had been to the clinic. She had had an ultrasound. She had tried pills. She had visited bush doctors. Some days were better than others and, for the most part, she went about her days and worked hard despite the pain. Today, even though the pain was especially intense, was no exception.

"Let's go."

"Are you sure? You can rest. We can wash tomorrow."

"No. It's okay. Let's go."

She rose carefully from the hammock and went to the far side of the house to gather her clean clothes in a small plastic bag. Her bucket of dirty clothes was already packed with a thick washing brush and a pack of powdered soap resting on top. She pulled the wooden doors of the house closed, picked up her bucket, and walked quickly along the small grass path in the opposite direction from which I'd come. I picked up my bucket and followed. I quickly caught up but fell behind again as the grass turned to mud as we neared the river. Walking on a wet mud path was a skill I was still mastering. It was with well-founded pride that I can claim that during my last year in Santa Cruz, I did not "drop" or slip and fall at all. "Dropping down" or slipping and falling, especially by the river, is considered very detrimental to health and a prominent mother in the village had just died the previous year after doing so. If I avoided dropping, I hoped I would avoid creating undue worry for my safety from my friends and neighbors in the village as well as avoid creating unnecessary amounts of muddy washing.

"You can wash here." She was pointing to a large flat rock at the river's edge at the end of a gently sloping embankment. She took the rock at the base of the steeper, muddier slope. Even with her illness, I was still more in need of washing assistance. I took off my flip flops and balanced my bucket between the rock and the embankment, gently slipping into the water. As I adjusted myself facing the rock, the cool river water eddied around my knees, slowly soaking several inches of the bottom of my skirt, creeping up, defying gravity. We both carefully unpacked our buckets, wetting the clothes and piling them next to the rock to wait their turn. We were alone at the river today. My schedule and her pain had put us about an hour behind the other ladies. One at a time each piece was soaped, scrubbed against the rock, and rinsed. We lost ourselves in the rhythm of the washing for a few minutes until she broke the silence.

"My husband says that maybe, if I still have the pain, we can go across or we can see the man who gets his bush medicine from across."

"Is that better than here?"

"Yes, it's different across. But there is a lady here, too, in San Antonio, she knows the bush medicine that is good for this problem."

"What do you think the problem is?"

"I don't know. From before, I was walking in the farm with my husband and I dropped. They said my womb opened. Maybe it got cold inside and it needs to get warm again."

We continued washing as I talked about how troubles getting pregnant were quite common in the U.S. and what some of the reasons for pain that I'd heard about in that context might be. It seemed like most of those reasons had been ruled out by the interventions she had tried. While I got the sense that her illness was not necessarily uncommon, it was more difficult to pinpoint the exact nature of it. We both hoped that the healer she mentioned, who was trained across the border in Guatemala, was able to provide the relief she had been seeking.

As part of her husband's extended family, she had encountered this healer before. Having moved to Santa Cruz from Guatemala a generation before, her husband's family had suffered a great loss the previous summer. His mother had entered the hospital for a hernia operation and died during the surgery. Intense sadness at their mother's unexpected loss overwhelmed the children. Sadness turned to an anger that was tearing the family apart. The healer was called but the treatment was never completed. The family's wellness has ebbed and flowed since, with her often caught in the middle.

Returning to her house after bathing, with our buckets heavy with wet, clean clothes, she invited me in to help bake tortillas for her husband's lunch. He would soon return from his farm where he had been checking on the progress of his corn. He would hope to get a good yield so he could sell the surplus and have money to pay for her treatment. Reluctantly, she paused for a few minutes when another wave of pains came but quickly returned to tending the fire.

"So, you think this healer can help?"

"Yes, he knows this sickness. I know a lady he helped. He knows the bush medicine from across and he knows it here."

"I hope your pain goes away soon." I was not surprised by the inconclusive nature of my friend's illness but I was hopeful that she would find relief with her latest attempt at healing. Only four miles from the newly opened, state-sponsored polyclinic, Santa Cruz residents often used the services there. The details of illnesses and treatments though are very often lost in translation. Seeking treatment ten miles in the other direction, over the Guatemala border, was sometimes considered a more attractive option, especially to those families with ties "across" and with the means to travel there. Different types of services, such as specialized surgeries, for example, are offered in Guatemala, and comparable services, injections, for example, are often less expensive there. "Bush doctors," however, are typically more expensive across but they are considered to be more knowledgeable and effective in treating serious illnesses.

My friend was able to seek treatment from the healer from the border town and was showing some improvement when the healer suffered an unfortunate accident and was confined to the hospital in Belize City for several months. My friend opted to continue treatment with bush medicine from another local healer and was satisfied with the results. She now has fewer days of intense pain. She still has not given birth to any children.

My friend's story illustrates how illness is incorporated in, and understood in the context of, both daily activities and the wider set of ecological and historical factors that shape these everyday practices. Her flexibility in terms of how she thinks about and goes about seeking treatment for her problem is echoed throughout my observations of illness in Santa Cruz. Her willingness to utilize the Belizean health care system, and her subsequent dissatisfaction with it, is common. Her understanding of the knowledge of healers with ties to Guatemala is also echoed throughout the village and her reference to the cold/hot as a factor in her illness also reflects this link.[1] Her husband's family's recent arrival in Belize, their loss of their mother, keeping her own house, her visiting the farm, the need to work, the family's current economic situation, the proximity to the cool creek; all of these factors contribute to the way she chooses to deal with her illness. In this chapter, I provide background to clarify how the convergence of these factors contributes to the understanding of wellness in Santa Cruz. History and politics play a role in shaping how ecological factors affect daily life. This background discussion illustrates how flexibility in response to an array of influences, from ecological changes and population flux to court rulings the changing availability of services, has been crucial in shaping Maya communities in Belize in general, and, more specifically, the study community.

SITUATING SANTA CRUZ

In many ways, Santa Cruz village is unique in the Toledo District. In terms of its pre-history, its soil quality and its current role in national and international land rights discussions, it might be well argued that it is unlike other nearby Maya villages. In many ways, however, it might be considered a typical Belizean Maya village. In terms of its everyday practices, its visual presentation, its residents' daily joys and struggles, it might be argued that it is quintessentially Maya. Located on the stretch of recently paved road connecting the Southern highway with the Guatemala border (notably, the road was unpaved in 2011 at the time of this study), Santa Cruz village is comprised of 76 households situated in small clusters, with extended families often sharing proximity. Most of these houses are visible from the road, with a few obscured by the "bush" or lowland forest that is cleared to build structures. None of the families live in the "high bush" or more than a few minutes' walk from the road, although many remember a time when they did live up to a several hours walk from the road. Only two households of the 76 officially listed did not keep a family farm as their primary means of subsistence. The vast majority of the male household heads practice farming as their primary work activity, with a much smaller number supplementing their farming practice with other outside work.

AGRICULTURE AND DAILY LIFE

When Thompson wrote about Maya communities in Toledo in 1930 that "their whole life centers on agriculture," he conveyed the observation that I also found to be true: that the details and nuances of daily social life grow from and are woven into the agricultural process. The residents of Santa Cruz use what have come to be known as "traditional" farming practices, or *milpa* agriculture. Maya communities living within lowland rainforest ecosystems have practiced what is known as "slash and burn" or swidden agriculture for over a thousand years. While current population and conservation pressures in the Toledo District have questioned the sustainability of this practice, given a stable population and a collective land management strategy, it is the most sustainable way to farm in this type of ecosystem. While Maya communities in northern Belize and throughout the Peten region of Guatemala and beyond have similar agricultural histories, their widely different socio-political histories in regards to indigenous land management have forced the waning of this land use strategy in much of the Maya world.

In Santa Cruz, shifting cultivation is the norm, with corn planting occurring twice a year, in May and December (or a week or so outside these months). For the May planting, or *k'ux*, high bush or old growth forest is chopped with machete, left to dry, and burned. For the December planting, or *matahambre*, areas of secondary growth are chopped and planting occurs without burning. While the size and location of individual farms are selected by individual farmers, community rules do exist; for example, areas closer to the village are left for older men. Plots are often between two and four manzana (a manzana equaling about an acre and a third) and are cleared and planted by individual farmers with cooperative assistance. After the harvest, plots are left to return to forest for soil nutrient regeneration and are not typically used for at least seven years, although there are differing reports about best practices versus actual practices. Again, the continued use of shifting cultivation is crucial to the structure of everyday social and economic life in Santa Cruz, with activities influenced by the timing of plantings and harvests.

Women and children also play a crucial role in the way agricultural and forest-collection activities form the structure of everyday life. While men prepare fields for planting, plant crops, maintain crops[2], harvest crops and, to a varying extent, collect wild plants, hunt wild animals and fish, women process and prepare crops for consumption and sale, and, to a varying extent, collect and process many wild plants. Species cultivated include both subsistence crops, such as corn and beans, and other crops more commonly grown for sale, such as rice and *pepitoria*. It should be noted that there is flexibility in subsistence versus cash crops. For example, bags of corn can be sold if money is needed and rice can be retained to be eaten by the family. Many families both eat and sell beans, and this flexibility applies to a variety of cultivated, semi-cultivated, and wild foods. Women are also primarily responsible for the care of domestic animals, most commonly chicken and pigs, which are fed corn and grown without chemical feed while being free, in most cases, to roam the village. In addition to processing and preparing food items, women are responsible for washing both clothes and dishes, most commonly accomplished in the river or creek closest to the family home. Caring for children also is a responsibility of women, with other siblings, both female and male, playing a large role in child care. Younger boys are often responsible for the gathering of firewood used for cooking on the firehearth. Children of all ages and both genders are frequently sent on other errands, to the corn mill or to the shop, for example. As extended formal education increases in popularity, children's work is sometimes taken on by older family members. Much of this work, again, is guided and structured by the land use cycles made possible by the land tenure system.

Not all neighboring villages continue the practice of shifting cultivation, or slash and burn agriculture, as it is limited by private landownership and it continues to be targeted by local environmental groups and popular scholars as a system of agricultural production that contributes to forest degradation (Diamond 2011). Understanding customary land tenure in Belize, and in Santa Cruz in particular, is crucial to understanding the implications of shifting agricultural practices to the history and future of Maya identity and heritage.

LAND AND LAND RIGHTS

In October 2007, Santa Cruz and Conejo, two Maya communities in Southern Belize, received a landmark court decision ruling that ostensibly gave them the rights to their lands in the first direct implementation of the 2007 UN Declaration of the Rights of Indigenous Peoples (Zarger 2009; Wainwright 2008). In order to come to the decision, the Chief Justice of the Belizean High Court interpreted the relevant constitutional provisions with reference to the preamble of the Belize Constitution, which requires "policies of state which protect . . . the identity, dignity and social and cultural values of Belizeans, including Belize's indigenous peoples" (Wainwright 2008). These rights, he found, "derive directly from indigenous customary land tenure are 'property' protected by the Constitution of Belize, in connection with the rights to equal protection and to life, liberty, security of the person and protection of the law" (Campbell and Anaya 2008: 377). Critically supported by affidavits from anthropologists and geographers working with contemporary Maya communities in southern Belize, as well as by local activist organizations representing the Maya communities, the land claim incorporated an expression of continuity in land use, of a historical connection to the land based on social identity, economic livelihood, and ecological knowledge. It is important to note that this decision, unlike the subsequent affirmation of the legal land rights of the remaining Maya villages in Toledo that was challenged and upheld in 2015 by the Caribbean High Court, has never been appealed. In an investigation of the background that contributed to this 2007 decision, in addition to what came after, it is important to understand that the formation of identity among Belizean Maya rests on the understanding and articulation of intersections between the ancient and the contemporary, the political and the ecological, and the broad and the particular as they relate to Maya life in southern Belize.

The effects of the land rights case on the shaping of heritage conceptions in Santa Cruz should not be underestimated. While there is no indication that daily work activities and land use changed through Santa Cruz's involvement in the landmark decision, the community members' exposure to information and ways of organizing and engaging with a larger political and economic system as a result of the legal process was significant, as was their articulation of their land use practice, which was something more commonly embodied than discussed. Weekly meetings with activists and scholars to discuss land management strategies and encourage the development of plan for future use and conservation of cultural and ecological heritage resources, sparked a new reflexive focus on how daily work was a manifestation of heritage practice. Additionally, the understanding of the similarities and differences between Belizean Maya groups and both Guatemalan Maya groups and other Belizean ethnic groups, including Creole, Garifuna, East Indian, and Mestizo, was drawn into focus. What it meant to be both "Belizean" and "Maya," was a consideration given increased saliency through the land rights engagement. While politicized terminology was not notably adopted by community members, the social and political climate created by Santa Cruz's centrality in these discussions of heritage and how that might play out in everyday lives was, and is, crucial to this discussion.

The testimony given in the high court affidavits point conclusively to extensive evidence, which demonstrates cultural-geographical continuity between the present Maya residents and pre-contact Maya communities (Wainwright 2007; Grandia 2007a; Wilk 2007). This is also well supported throughout the ethnographic and archaeological literatures as well as throughout my research. There is a southern Belizean continuity in Maya agricultural practice and its resultant social implications in the household across time and (limited) space. Part of this continuity, notably, is in the documented flexibility and variability within the Mopan and Q'eqchi' communities. This discussion shows that, like indigenous communities in "developing" countries throughout the world, the Belizean Maya are certainly subject to the political and economic pressures of globalizing forces; however, their ability to utilize strategies adapted from past and present practices in times of change has allowed them to maintain a distinct and consistent identity.

Development projects are a major conduit of land use change. Wainwright (2007: 7) offers a kind of updated Marxist deconstruction of development, examining the ways in which development by way of capitalist encroachment has played out among the Maya in southern Belize. In his historical account, he stresses the invention and creation of accepted realities related to Belizeaness or Mayaness or *milpa* agriculture (Wainwright 2008). Changing political boundaries and ideologies, as well as efforts like the *Maya Atlas* (Toledo Alcaldes Association 1997) played a significant role in the past in demarcating territories under the jurisdiction and use by certain groups. Before the land right decision, many scholars framed land use issues among the Maya in southern Belize as contentious (Robbins et al. 2010). Preliminary studies indicate that the high court ruling has not eliminated this confusion and negotiation and demarcation of land between villages continues (Wainwright and Bryan 2009), adding to further constructions of identity. Defining what village one is from, where one's family hailed from, and how you understand what one's ancestors were doing with the land all contribute to these identity definitions and, consequently, heritage constructions.

These complexities call for a more detailed awareness of nuance and the ways in which the effects of these changes and development initiatives play out in the daily practices of the Maya of southern Belize. Understanding how individuals embody these changes, and how this actually affects what people do, is beneficial and is hopefully what is provided with this study. Maya communities have a documented creative and adaptive capacity for responding to change when faced with strong pressures from outside and more dominant societies. This is evident in the pragmatic and fluid ways in which individuals interact with their environments, which reflect both years of development pressure and years of resistance through continuity. An investigation of pragmatic practice in the face of certain ecological stimuli illuminates the "mosaic" (Robbins et al. 2010) of ways in which individuals respond to changes in their environment. In her discussion of the profound effects of Hurricane Iris on the landscape of southern Belize, Zarger (2009: 144) conceptualizes another impetus for further variation in ecological interaction as an "aperture," noting, "not just a gap or discontinuity, the spaces created by the event served as a pivotal opening for a change in dynamics of control over the landscape." Through this statement, we are provided with an example of how environmental change and politico-economic pressures play out in ways that diverge from more unidirectional political ecological models of environmental and cultural change in response to development.

This desire to focus on the particulars of how the convergence of the politics and economics of development shape individual and group identity has been a welcome focus of a handful of scholars working with the Maya in Belize. Zarger's (2009) paper is important in that it illustrates, through the very immediate and tangible example of food, that the environmental, social, and political factors that are salient for the Mopan and Q'eqchi' Maya, as Belizeans, are distinct from those important to Maya communities in Mexico or Guatemala, where political histories and national identities are markedly different. Medina (1998) makes the observation that Maya claims of indigenous status are challenged more frequently in Belize than in neighboring countries. She adds that this has encouraged a linguistic kinship between Mopan and Q'eqchi' Maya communities in Belize and those in Guatemala. One lesson from Guatemala, perhaps, received through the lens of a long-standing Maya interaction with the land, is reflected in the observation that "any subsistence outlet in the indigenous economy is generally preferable than wage labor" (Grandia 2007b). Zarger (2009) notes the increasing practice of Q'eqchi' and Mopan men returning to subsistence farming from wage labor after being faced with the high cost of buying food for their families. This is an important point of focus, with these studies essentially arguing against a development assumption that subsistence agriculture is somehow less desirable than wage labor or other more modern forms of agriculture, illustrating a fundamental problem with a unidirectional and linear modernization narrative. An anonymous reviewer criticized Crooks (1997), who explores biocultural models in hopes of understanding how changing environmental conditions affect school achievement in a Mopan Maya village for issues of characterizing farmers' lives as unsatisfying. It is telling, too, that the Belizean High Court needed to be informed about

Maya agriculture as relevant in the present and characterized by a tangible ecological, social, intellectual, spiritual, and economic logic (Grandia 2007a) and, indeed, that land rights affirmed through the recent legal court processes continue to be challenged at all levels from a variety of actors in the Belizean socio-political landscape.

An example of the dynamic and fluid nature of customary Maya land use that has been explored by several authors is the use of cash crops alongside subsistence agriculture, which has been framed as historically contentious (Campbell and Anaya 2008). There is a centuries-old waxing and waning of cash crop usage that has existed alongside the *milpa* system (Wilk 1991). These studies may render Steinberg's (2002) observation that cacao is a representation of the larger change in Mopan culture from local and more subsistence oriented to global and more market-oriented over-simplistic, especially in regard to how these changes might affect daily life. Focusing on a more pragmatic and flexible relationship, Zarger (2009: 141) points out that Maya farmers have, at times, been "more and less reliant on cash crops in response to changing power dynamics, exploitive regimes, forced labor, and available land."

There exists a degree of nuance and flexibility to Maya land use patterns and their resultant social systems that are widely documented (Wilk 1991), but may not be immediately obvious to those working in the frame of unidirectional development modeling. Indeed, Gaskins (2003) in her extensive work in a Yucatec Maya community noted that the transition from "corn to cash," contrary to popular assumptions, did not lead to fundamental culture change (Gaskins 2003). It is important to note that many scholars stress the ability of local agencies to confront the encroachment of globalizing forces, emphasizing the need to move past a simple "traditional versus modern" dichotomy to consider how social behavior changes in response to changing ecological conditions (Grandia 2007b; Zarger 2009; Wilk 1991). "We cannot not desire development" (Wainwright 2008: 10), but we can discuss how it is negotiated by the actors involved. The "we" in his argument points to scholars and readers, engaging them in this development dilemma, whereas there is a need, I would argue, for an inclusion of the Maya themselves in the we. "The developer" and "the Maya" are subject positions Wainwright (2008) shows to be constructed (Danziger 1996). In a very clear sense, Wainwright (2008) illuminates we are all developers: anthropologists, activists, the Maya themselves.

Zarger (2009) addresses this lack of nuance found in many development critiques, providing tangibility to Wainwright's development aporia. She notes that shifts in Maya agricultural practices, from farming to buying food, for example, are not indications of a "a unidirectional progression in the sense that traditional modernization studies have imagined" (Zarger 2009: 131). Grandia (2007a), in her affidavit to the Belizean high court, makes an important economic observation regarding land tenure, noting that "customary land management is not static or anti-market . . . it allows communities to make timely decisions about how to adjust their land management in response to new market opportunities and constraints." Wilk (1991) makes a similar point about the flexibility and resultant economic sustainability of traditional Maya land tenure systems. At the same time, continuity of land use among the Belizean Maya, particularly the Mopan in Santa Cruz, is a unique feature of environmental practice and social organization, as well as being crucial to personal identity and political positioning. Maya agricultural practices have changed very little in the past 150 years (Wainwright 2007: 8). In contrast with many Maya groups in Mexico and Guatemala (Goldin 1994), Belizean Maya communities have been less affected by colonial displacement and subsequent private land acquisition. Largely avoiding European-type lease or grant system also avoids an intensive disparity in wealth and capital, which disrupts customary social networks and belief systems (Grandia 2007b). While Santa Cruz has avoided this system, leaders in other Maya communities I spoke with frequently noted the difficulties in balancing leased land systems with customary social practices.

In Santa Cruz, everyday land use practices, a walk in the "bush" for example, take on additional importance in this context. Both the Mopan and Q'eqchi' Maya make use of forest species for subsistence in a frequent and varied way (Grandia 2007b, Zarger 2002). The antiquity of Maya ethnobotanical knowledge in Belize is understudied among both the Mopan and the contemporary Q'eqchi' although studies do point to an extensive use among this latter group (Grandia 2007b; Anderson et al. 2005; Leatherman and Goodman 2005). In their conclusion to their consensus ethnobotanical review, Bourbonnas-Spear et al. (2005: 335) note that despite "great changes in their way of life as a result of development . . . there is a re-awakening and greater interest in cultural matters," especially among young people. These "cultural matters" include the use of plants for both subsistence and medicinal purposes. This stimulation of cultural interest is multi-layered, with references to the archaeological past playing an active role. The following section considers this archaeological role.

PREHISTORIES

My interest in Santa Cruz, and the intersection of ecological heritage and wellness as it plays out there, was derived from this complex convergence of ecological, social, and political histories. However, it was both sparked and facilitated by the presence of *Uxb'enk'a,* or "old city," a Classic Period (AD 250–800) ancient Maya center located within the boundary of Santa Cruz. Forming a large portion of the collaborative research project of which I was a part, archaeological researchers, my colleagues, were present in the village and the surrounding forest working closely with the men of Santa Cruz to excavate and investigate many areas of the larger archaeological site. The interest in the lives of the ancient Maya ancestors, and, to some extent, their continuities with the current Maya residents of the same ecological space, was an undoubted driving force in both researcher and community involvement in the project as a whole.

Prior to my involvement with the project, focus had been placed explicitly on the role of archaeology and archaeological sites in communities, particularly Santa Cruz, through an "ethnography of archaeology" undertaken by Parks (2009). Parks was also responsible for the development and implementation of cultural heritage lessons, which focused on local archaeological findings, archaeological methodologies, and the role of the community in archaeological investigations. Together with PIs Zarger and Prufer, she also contributed to the development of a plan to broaden heritage conceptions through the curriculum, which provides illustrations and links between environmental and cultural practices (Zarger, Parks, and Prufer 2008; Baines and Zarger 2012).

This early call for attention to the intersections between environmental and cultural heritage considered local perceptions of both the ancient Maya sites and their surrounding landscapes (Zarger et al. 2008). While the aspects of daily life that are fundamentally different for today's residents of this stretch of land play a crucial role in my research, this multilayered focus on the Mayan past should not be ignored. In order to understand how ecological heritage is embodied through practice, understanding that "the kinds of heritage that are officially recognized and conserved by government organizations, also tend to be those with less meaning for people in their daily lives" (Howard 2003: 53) is an important piece. Research into Maya prehistory informs this discussion and, ultimately, the research presented in the subsequent chapters of this book.

The Maya civilization of the past has long captivated the interest of both scholars and the popular imagination far beyond Mesoamerica. The contemporary Maya are affected by this interest in numerous ways and their interactions with both archaeologists and the archaeological "data" they produce are, in many respects, instrumental to shaping identity and, in some cases, their daily lives. The nature of this intersection has become increasingly important among the contemporary Maya in Belize and those advocates and scholars working with them. Archaeological research, along with the physical archaeological sites and their place in the landscape form "active archaeoscapes" (Parks 2010) that local people, and a variety of other stakeholders, have an interest in accessing, studying, revering, or developing (Wilk 1985). As active knowledge, archaeology is a powerful tool and archaeological scholars have an important contribution to make toward the understanding of both cultural and ecological heritage constructions among current Maya populations.

Ancient Maya agriculture, and its complimentary political economic system, can be seen as an example of great success with a 2000-year legacy extended into the present-day Maya practice or a complete failure by comparison to the current system—this is a matter of opinion more than of data collection (Pyburn 1996). For our purposes here, attempting to tease out the details of these perceived successes and failures and how those relate to contemporary Maya life is a useful exercise. What Pyburn (1996) and Faust (2001) do not emphasize here is that opinion is, of course, shaped by objective. That is to say, in this case, the success or failure of the ancient Maya can be emphasized depending on how this relates to contemporary Maya ecological or social practice. In the same respect, continuity or discontinuity with the contemporary Maya can be emphasized or de-emphasized in this same way, depending on one's objective in shaping connections between current communities and a history of success or failure.

Broad discussions about the interrelation between environmental and cultural change invariably include a discussion of Maya environmental conservation versus overexploitation (Pyburn 1996; Faust 2001) with a controversial focus on overpopulation being a contributing force in the "fall" of Mayan civilization. The connection between land and soil degradation through overuse leading to environmental destruction and eventual ancient Maya collapse is a theory credited by many scholars to Meggers (1954). Environmental degradation theories of Maya collapse continued to gain popularity in the 1970s with theories of ancient Maya agricultural overexploitation and rhetoric focused on balance between the social and natural environment (Wilk 1985). Traditionally, scholars accepted and perpetuated that the Maya Lowlands were a harsh and fragile environment, able to support only a sparse population dependent on slash-and-burn agriculture (Wilk 1985; Faust 2001; Fedick and Morrison 2004). Dense populations, however, are not necessarily an explanation for over-exploitation of an environment (Fedick and Morrison 2004). Speaking to broader issues of environmental degradation, Emery (2007: 192) claims "the zooarchaeological record shows that despite more than 4,000 years of Maya hunting, forest clearance, and other forms of landscape modification, there is no evidence of extinctions or local extirpation of fauna." Scarborough (2003) points out an important disjunction in relation to Lowland Maya archaeology. Family farms persist in a settlement area that is less dense, creating an incongruity with the model of overpopulation and land degradation preceding a large-scale collapse. Overexploitation does not seem to be an archaeological reality, even if it continues to persist in popular rhetoric (Diamond 2011).

While care should be taken not to conflate discussions of statal collapse with those critiques relating directly to land use among individual farmers, perhaps a more considered approach to landscape modification and adaptation would be helpful in this discussion. Pyburn (1998) suggests that the transformation of landscapes has rarely been seen in mutualistic terms and "the capacity of stateless societies to significantly transform landscapes was often downplayed or denied." Scholars point to an increasing interest and focus on the micro-level variability of agricultural techniques and technologies among the ancient Maya peasant classes (Cliggett and Pool 2008: 2). The socioeconomic and sociopolitical organization of early complex societies changes with their landscapes (Dunning et al. 1998; Dunning and Beach 2000; Fedick 1996; Morehart and Helmke 2008). Following this logic, intensive Maya family farms probably were adapted to more than one type of political economy (Scarborough 2003). The variation and nuanced complexities of land use strategies in the ancient Maya Lowlands has been well documented (Pyburn 1998). Yet, still, the overpopulation/degradation/collapse model of Maya history and subsequent inheritance persists. This is fueled in large part, it might be argued, by pan-Maya identity activist movements that conflate Maya histories, as well as, as Wainwright (2008) suggests, by development initiatives.

Dunham et al. (2009) present new archaeological evidence to suggest that the southern Maya Mountains were an area rich with people using many intensive agricultural strategies to sustain themselves. This focus on variation and complexity in land use strategies has potentially potent implications for the intersection of Maya identity and development ideology surrounding land use. Wainwright (2008: 81) deconstructs a two-part framing of the Maya as ineffectual farmers in need of development assistance. First, he explains how the Maya are inextricably linked to *milpa* farming as part of the construction of their ethnic identity. Next, *milpa* farming is framed as destructive and environmentally unsustainable. This critique of the "Maya" farming system can be traced back through the archaeological literature, as described above, as well as through current popular and ethnographic literature, with the Maya being framed as responsible for the degradation of their environment and, ultimately, their social collapse.

Focusing on the landscape, the connection between economics and the study of space and place is well documented (Cliggett and Pool 2008: 5) but is newly being reconceived in terms of dynamic landscapes formed by both the mental and the material. In this sense, "all landscapes . . . are conceived and debated" (Cligget and Pool 2008: 6). This observation is salient in this discussion, with the formation of Maya identity closely linked to historic, but dynamic, landscapes. Archaeological sites might be seen as static material fixtures of the Belizean landscape, yet they take on a conceptual meaning in terms of identity and practice in contemporary Maya communities. Wainwright and Bryan (2009) compare land use and management from the Classic Maya period through to the present, noting that the Maya have managed resources, developed some technologies, adopted and modified others, attempting to adapt to environmental changes over time. They emphasize that existing local knowledge and technology have guided perceptions of both environmental change and alternative responses to it. The diversity of the lowland landscape over time is well-documented (Faust 2001). It follows, then, that a diversity of agricultural practice and a diversity of social organization would be probable. The dynamic nature of this "mosaic landscape" (Fedick and Morrison 2004) supports the existence of fluid social and ecological system.

As a model for economic organization in the Maya Lowlands, the "mosaic" or the recognition of a diversity of production activities and a complexity of resource distributions (Fedick and Morrison 2004; Dunning et al. 1998; Zarger 2009; Grandia 2007b), represents a more realistic picture of interacting households bound together through complex webs. This focus on diversity and complexity goes a certain distance in addressing the problematic nature of the archaeological practice as exemplified in many Belizean studies, with broad implications for the construction of contemporary Maya identity. Household data, including data regarding the positions of households within broader political economic landscapes, can be used to track and interpret regional-scale social, political, and economic changes. While keeping focus on the complexity of household-level web of interaction, Pyburn (1998) makes a case for cautious use of household studies. Maya smallholders "can exist within a variety of political and economic systems [and] their ubiquity in the Maya Lowlands may explain why household studies often fail to detect political or economic change at a macro level" (Pyburn 1998). An exploration of the intersection between the macro- and micro-level is crucial to understanding how an understanding of the past can permeate the Maya lives in the present.

Archaeologists believe that there is an active connection between the past and the present, which is relevant and has a positive social role to play in contemporary life (Wilk 1985). This role is an example of the construction of the particulars of cultural heritage. Archaeologists, too, have grappled with defining heritage in a way that makes the study of the past beneficial for the communities who have a distinct stake in it. Noting that it is a "conceptual box . . . and thus as much a human artifact as any of the individual things that comprise it" (Carman 2003: viii), archaeological discussions of heritage fall into three broad categories: commentary, research, and guides to practice (Carman 2003). The latter category seems to have employed with a particular emphasis in Belize. Medina (1998) emphasizes the impetus for the construction of Maya identity as involvement in growing tourism initiatives, with preHispanic sites of the Maya region having become major symbols for the alleviation of poverty for local communities (Parks 2010). This factor, it can be argued, is overstated in a consideration of the complexities involved in identity construction, however, Parks (2010: 441) also concludes, "there is no indication that the residents of Santa Cruz have a privileged understanding of the ancient Maya based on their indigenous identity as Maya people."

While this may be true in the sense of a specific historical event and ritual practice, however, it can be argued, as it was in the 2007 affidavits to the Belizean high court, that the understanding and connection between the ancient and contemporary Maya comes through land use strategies. "Ethnicity is a fluid category, as many Maya groups share similar cultural traits and have all descended from a common lineage that connects them all to the ancient Maya peoples who inhabited Mesoamerica before the arrival of Europeans" (Grandia 2007a). More specifically, contemporary community norms, it is observed, are derived "from a broader normative system shared by all the Maya in southern Belize" (Campbell and Anaya 2008: 377). This linkage between the ecological and the social in the frame of "Mayaness," it can be argued, is not only pragmatic in a political and economic sense, but is also a tangible connection based on archaeological and ethnographic evidence about the nature of farming and forest use.

ECOLOGIES

Life in Santa Cruz is explicitly shaped by the unique ecologies of southern Belize. The Toledo District receives more than 4,000-mm rainfall per year, which is among the highest in the Maya region and compares to 2,500 mm in the Petén region of Guatemala and 700 mm in the Yucatan peninsula of Mexico (Kennett et al. 2012; Ridley et al. 2015). The majority of this rainfall occurs in what is commonly referred to as the rainy season, from May to January and dictates the seasonal corn planting cycles within the neotropical lowland rainforest as described earlier. This high rainfall allows for shifting cultivation without the development of irrigation systems.

Archaeologists seeking to understand the development and occupation of the ancient site of *Uxb'enk'a* located within the boundary of Santa Cruz lands have identified an unusually fertile 25-km long hilly relief feature, which extends from the foothills of the Maya Mountains to the north to coastal plain in the south (Hammond 1975; Prufer et al. 2011). Local reports of the increased soil fertility in this area are supported by the presence of underlying bedrock, which is layered mudstone and sandstone (Keller et al. 2003; Thompson and Prufer 2015). Rapid pedogensis and high soil fertility in conjunction with the high rainfall create an ideal ecological scenario for the success of agriculture without intensification. While areas of high and low soil fertility do factor into the areas farmed, actual crop yields are determined by a convergence of multiple factors, including weather, farmer experience, and intercropping in addition to soil type (Culleton 2012).

It is worthwhile noting again here that *milpa* agriculture in lowland rainforest ecosystems is an ecologically sustainable practice given the norm of shifting cultivation. While the practice has been compromised and rendered unsustainable throughout the Maya region with combinations of private landownership and clear-cutting of land for larger scale agricultural practices, Santa Cruz's land management strategies and ecological systems have been successful in sustaining it. Santa Cruz manages a mosaic landscape of shifting agricultural plots with rapid forest regeneration and vegetation growth. Evidence for this has been recently provided using Light Detection and Ranging (LIDAR), a remote sense technique (Prufer et al. 2015), adding imaging to the current and historic accounts of landscape use in this region.

HISTORIES

Understanding life and land use in Santa Cruz today is dependent on recognizing the colonial legacy of resource extraction in the Toledo district. Belize has a well-documented history of timber harvesting for export to European markets beginning in the 1660s when the British began to cut logwood. Young, Toledo and Company was founded in 1839, as the colony became known as British Honduras, and it became the largest logging company in southern Belize. The company went bankrupt well before the turn of the 20th century as the trees that were easily assessable for harvest were depleted, however, by that time, several permanent settlements had been created (Binford 2007; Wilk 1991) and the colony of British Honduras was firmly established.

Belize was granted internal self-governance in 1964 and gained independence in 1981. Its colonial history of slavery and indentured servitude in lumber camps and, subsequently, sugar plantations, coupled with indigenous populations and more recent arrivals, has left it with an ethnically diverse population: Maya, Creole, Garifuna, Mestizo, East Indian, Mennonite, Chinese, and others. Of the 32 Maya languages comprising six language families recognized throughout the Maya region, Belize is home to three: Mopan, Q'eqchi', and Yucatec. While Mopan and Yucatec are in the same language family, Q'eqchi' is linguistically dissimilar. The Toledo District is home to primarily Mopan and Q'eqchi' speakers, while Yucatec speakers make their home further north in the country, close to the Yucatan peninsula of Mexico.

While there is a politicized element to the tracing of Belizean Maya histories and the writing of exact migration patterns are based on "skimpy sources" (Wilk 2007), there is both academic and local agreement that direct ancestors of both the Mopan and Q'eqchi' Maya were settled in the Toledo district of Belize in the pre-contact period and were forcibly relocated to Guatemala by the Spanish during the 16th century. While borders were loose and migration was common, they organized a formal return to Belize in the 1880s (Grandia 2007a). While Maya ethnicity maintains a certain amount of fluidity, Mopan, referred to often as simply "Maya," and Q'eqchi' are distinguished in Toledo, though there are frequent intermarriages and bilingualism and trilingualism with English, are common. Ties to Guatemala (through family, through economic relationships) reflect this history of fluidity. While Grandia (2007b) notes, "Q'eqchi' residents of Toledo clearly assert their national allegiance as citizens of Belize, yet they maintain ties and affinities with a broader Q'eqchi' community, as well as a broader pan-Maya movement," care should be taken not to conflate all Q'eqchi' communities. Albeit to a lesser extent, my research found this to be the case in primarily Mopan Maya communities, Santa Cruz for example. While just 11 of the 76 families have a primarily Q'eqchi'-speaking head of household, many other community members also speak Q'eqchi' as a second or third language. My research supports caution not to overstate the fluidity between these Maya ethnicities, noting a detectable social distinction between them (such as "he does it that way because he's a Q'eqchi'" when referring to distinctive farming practices, for example), however, there is a broader cohesion between them when faced with pan-Maya issues, particularly those related to land use and land rights, which have become increasingly salient in the past decade.

MOVING FORWARD

Teasing out much continuity, as well as the significant changes, in Maya identity and ecological practice in southern Belize is an ongoing process. Ethnographers have shown that some answers are to be found in the particulars of daily life, noting consistency and variation within and between households and villages. I would argue, again, that too little attention has been paid to the processes involved in both how things change and, indeed, how they perpetuate. Extrapolating across temporal and spatial boundaries seems less likely to reify "Mayaness" if we focus on processes rather than particulars. Bringing in a discussion of the body and wellness helps promote this focus and, hopefully, further understand how identity is derived from perceptions of history, politics, and local ecology by illuminating the lived daily experience of the community members. Santa Cruz, and the practices and perceptions of its community members, is consistently responding to changes. Current negotiations of flux include the practical and political ramifications of paving the road through the village and oil prospecting in the surrounding community lands. I provide mention of these current events as illustrations of how events and processes call heritage constructions into sharp focus. In the following chapters I present data, analyses, and discussion to address this absence and further explore the ways in which heritage might be understood as integral to wellness through its manifestation in everyday environmental interactions and practice.

While considering these data, I would encourage the reader to continue to recognize, in light of the background presented here, that the term "heritage" was chosen carefully for its weight: its incorporation of intangibility, commodification, performance, and the association of colonization. It is a loaded term and, because of this, allows for fluid definition. Chambers (2006: 2) states, "Over the last couple of centuries or so, the most significant thing about heritage has not been what it might come to represent, but rather who gets to represent it and to what intent." I accept the problematic nature of this term and bring it back to an investigation of the phenomenological experience of those living in the shadow of the representations of heritage, the residents of Santa Cruz. By bringing the individual body back into heritage discussions, this research provides a contribution to a discussion about wellness and the politics of health. Exploring and analyzing the links between heritage constructions, ecological heritage practices, and wellness, provides a critique of heritage politics and new considerations for the future of the Belizean Maya land use. At the time of printing, it is clear that the complex convergence of the historical, ecological, and political factors discussed here are not static, and Santa Cruz faces an uncertain future in this regard.

NOTES

1. Maya humoral medical conceptions, including hot/cold references, are discussed in more detail in the next chapter. Much of the documentation of these references comes from studies undertaken in Guatemala; however, there are significant studies discussing similar concepts, which were undertaken in Mexico. Little systematic work has been done on this topic in Belize and my study did not uncover any significant data on this topic beyond anecdotal references similar to that described here.

2. In Santa Cruz, fields are typically prepared without the use of chemical fertilizers. Chemical herbicides, such as gramazone, are sometimes used for weed control or "cleaning" of the fields, if they can be afforded and if labor and time needed for chopping weeds is limited.

There was a flurry of discussion among the men. I knew enough Mopan to pick out a few of the words that were being volleyed back and forth. A few weeks earlier, a close friend had described her pale skinned visitor, flush from the heat, as *muk'a'an*. This had been a compliment; her ruddy cheeks made her look "healthy" my friend explained. *Muk'a'an* was a good word for healthy, but it also meant "strong." The flush of her cheeks made her seem like she had been working hard and to do hard work, one had to be strong. The root, *muk*, was the word for "muscle." Apolonio broke off from the discussion and offered a sentence: *K'u wich walach o bet ti ketch ti muk'a'anetch?* The other men weighed in, offering different sentence structures and alternate words. Mopan, I was learning, offered much flexibility in its spoken expression and the sorts of questions I was hoping to ask, in the language of scientific inquiry, were not common.

"It has a lot of meaning," Basilio asserted thoughtfully about the sentence in question.

"A lot of hard work, taking care of myself, eating *caldo* . . ." he continued. The other men agreed, discussing the possible meanings and responses wrapped up in question as they related to how it should be asked. They reached a relative consensus, and Apolonio's translation of "what makes a healthy person?" became the question that formed the base of my preliminary interviews and free list requests (the results of which are presented later in this chapter). Learning the nuances of the Mopan ways of describing wellness, however, had only just begun.

"How about if I want to ask if the corn is healthy?" *Muk'a'an*, with my limited understanding, seemed like a good word to use to describe the corn. If it is healthy and strong it would be able to withstand winds and pests.

Laughter erupted amongst the men. Corn is not *muk'a'an*, only people are *muk'a'an*. If the corn is good, you can say it is *kich'pan*. I knew this word. It was frequently used throughout the village. It described tortillas and new skirts and freshly brushed hair. It meant "pretty." Often, as my baking skills improved, someone would enter a kitchen when I was making tortillas and exclaim, "*Kristina! Kich'pan wah!*" admiring my pretty tortilla and, also, I was now realizing, giving me an indication of the weight of the word through its association with corn tortillas, which are the accepted, most important staple. If a family had nothing else to eat, they would eat tortillas. I witnessed this many times. Learning to make tortillas well, or "pretty tortillas," was an incredibly important step in my acceptance in and understanding of the experience of daily life in Santa Cruz.

Kich'pan, I had come to learn, also was used to mean "clean" and I came to confirm that any obvious connection between cleanliness and prettiness that might be expected from this overlap did actually exist. And now, with plants at least, being healthy became part of this triad.

Pretty corn was healthy corn and healthy corn was clean corn. In order to ensure a healthy crop of corn, men spent many hours "cleaning" their fields, chopping the weeds and the underbrush to ensure enough space and resources for the corn plants. Some farmer in the village had taken to using herbicides to make "cleaning" easier and I wondered if this practice might one day affect the terminology used. Could corn "cleaned" with herbicides be as "healthy?" Is it all *kich'pan*? While I never found a definitive answer to this question, the use of herbicides did not seem to prevent the corn from being *kich'pan*.

My next lesson in the meaning of *"kich'pan"* came on a bus while returning from the wedding held in a Q'eqchi' village about a two-hour drive away. The bride had many relatives in Santa Cruz and the bus had been provided to enable their attendance. I sat by the window and Rosaria sat next to me on the small bench seat of the decommissioned U.S. school bus. Although she spoke Mopan to her family in Santa Cruz, Q'eqchi' was her first language and, today, as was often the case, she spoke to me in English.

"That corn is beautiful," she said as she pointed across my lap at the field at the side of the road as we passed.

"Why?" I was still wondering what made a field beautiful or pretty. Or healthy. Or clean.

"The corn is beautiful because it takes the sun and rain and gives us energy. Indian people, we need energy to work, for our life." I nodded as I looked out the window. We were on the other side of a series of hills that separated Santa Cruz and the road to the border from this flatter landscape. In Santa Cruz, it would be unusual to be able to see such a large cornfield so close to the road.

"That rice is beautiful," she was pointing again, as I refocused, I saw that the cornfield had given way to a considerably shorter grassy expanse of rice plants. Again, this was an unusual sight from the road.

"Why?"

"The rice is beautiful because we sell it and it gives us money to buy soap, sugar, salt." Rosaria continued to explain how both crops were *kich'pan*, or beautiful, as she translated in English, and, as she explained how, a clearer picture of how food is connected to wellness through Mopan vocabulary began to emerge. Just as the UKAA executive had told me, wellness terms have "a lot of meaning." When a field is healthy, or *kich'pan*, it is not simply looking lush, producing a good yield, or growing well, but it is also providing a means for its owners to be well, both directly, through nourishment and the resultant ability to work, and indirectly, through the sale of the crops to provide the cash needed for essential supplies. A beautiful field, in this sense, equals a healthy life. Using this same term, *kich'pan*, to describe plants as healthy, pretty, and clean is illustrative and an indicator of the integral nature of agricultural practice to wellness conceptions.

"People are healthy when the corn is healthy." It was later that same week and my conversation with Delphina had turned from a discussion of wellness terminology to a discussion of wellness relationships. She went on to imply that the converse, then, was also true. When the corn is sick, people are sick. Both, in Mopan, are *k'oha'an*. Although a broad term for sickness, *k'oha'an* was used most commonly in my wellness conversations when there was a perception of a specific illness origin. General feelings of un-wellness were more likely to be described as someone feeling *ma k'in wool* or not well/not happy. Interestingly, corn can correctly be described as *k'in wool* or feeling well/happy. For example, when it rains, the corn is happy. Apart from facilitating my enjoyment at having something relevant to say beyond "it's raining!" while dashing from house to house during afternoon visits in the rainy season, understanding how to say that corn is happy helped me further understand how some domains might be flexibly delineated, depending on the context. While plants could be, and were, thought about as feeling in a way that would be reserved for humans using English (Baines and Zarger 2012), they could not be described as healthy and strong in the same way. With this increased understanding of the vocabulary of wellness (Table 3.1), I proceeded to delve more systematically into the definition and flexibility of these domains. During this process, the importance of food, and the practice of acquiring what was described as traditional food, to the development of heritage and maintenance of wellness became increasingly apparent.

INDIAN PEOPLE EAT CORN

Making observations and participating in activities and conversations with corn as the focus was inevitable in Santa Cruz. Corn is the pivot around which daily activities occur. Planting, tending, processing, and preparing: work, in large part, is related to the plant. Any cursory history of Maya agriculture would have prepared me for this revelation, with

Table 3.1.   Wellness vocabulary: adjectives

Mopan	English	Descriptive uses
muk'a'an	healthy, strong	people
kich'pan	pretty, healthy, clean	plants, people, animals, inanimate objects
k'oha'an	sick	people, plants, animals
k'in wool	happy/well	people, plants, animals
ma k'in wool	not happy/not well	people, plants, animals
nohan en wool	satisfied, comfortable	people

corn celebrated as "the sacred staff of life" (Messer 1987) or the "mother" of the Maya in various incarnations, from the Popul Vuh to historic documents to artistic representations. How the omnipresence of corn was reflected in the thoughts and practices of the Maya residents of Santa Cruz was of continued interest to me as I sought to understand being well in the village.

"Our corn is our corn and we cannot forget that." Basilio was often keen to emphasize an understanding, and pride, in his being part of a Maya community. His statement reflects this. Pride in being Maya means embracing corn. Depending on it, making a living from it, made you *nohan en wool* or "satisfied." Over the course of our many conversations, he spoke freely about corn from multiple perspectives: as tradition, as political activism and, most commonly, as a means to keeping the body well. He talked about how Maya bodies were different from mine, about how they needed corn to stay *muk'a'an*, to work hard. Eating corn was important, he made clear, but only part of the traditional practices, which include respecting all the abstentions and ritual practices associated with planting, harvesting, and preparing corn.

"If we don't do these things, if we don't understand about our corn, we will have sickness, we cannot live in a good way," he explained. He spoke about Maya bodies with both a spiritual reverence and an acute biological understanding, as if these perspectives were seamlessly integrated. Although his passion and eloquence were unusual, his perspective was echoed in many of the conversations throughout my time in Santa Cruz. The connection between traditional foods, and traditional ways of producing and gathering foods and being a well "Maya" person frequently came to light. This was evident in everyday ethnographic encounters and focused illness interactions, like that relayed at the beginning of this chapter, as well as emerging as an important finding in the collection of the free lists.

Free Lists

When asked to list "the important things to be a healthy person" respondents[5] answered so frequently with traditional foods that I revisited my Mopan translation of the question to be sure that there was nothing inherent in the question to lead people to think that I was looking for food responses. Assured that my prompt was adequately broad, I continued with the collection and, after 50 free lists had been recorded and the 68 different responses (of a total of 288 individual responses) were analyzed, I found that only 10 did not reference food.

Of the 50 respondents, the most frequent response (n = 22) was *kich'pan hanal* or "healthy/clean/good food." The nuances of the word *kich'pan* were discussed in detail in the previous section, and the meanings of the phrase are additionally complex. While further questioning (*what kinds of foods are kich'pan hanal?*) and pile sorting analyses (details presented later in this chapter) revealed that foods gathered from the bush and subsistence staples produced on the family's farm were most often considered *kich'pan hanal*, there were cases when packaged foods from the shop could be considered *kich'pan* in the sense that they were clean and pretty in their sealed packages. With that caution in mind, it is important to note that, of the 58 food-related responses, no store-bought items were mentioned individually. Every food item mentioned by more than two respondents was either a gathered food or a traditional Maya staple, with the exception of stout beer.

Many gathered foods represented in this table of responses are culturally significant plants and, as these responses became more frequent, I made the decision to collect an additional free list to explore this plant relationship further. In this data collection, respondents[6] were asked to name plants that were "important to life." Of the 55 total plants listed, only nine did not have primary food-related uses. Twenty-one were cultivated plants, 33 were local wild plants gathered in the forests surrounding Santa Cruz, including both top responses, local palms pacaya (*ch'ib*) and jippy jappa (*käla*). One response (*tutu* or jute) was a local fresh water snail gathered for food. Of note when considering these data are the significantly higher numbers of unique responses in proportion to the number of respondents. From this it can be gleaned that there are a large number of plants that are considered important and there is less agreement about the importance of these plants than with the healthy items in the previous list.

During both free list collections and ensuing discussions, I often heard gathered and hunted foods and traditionally cultivated foods referred to as "our food" or "the food Maya people eat." In the context of the first free list, statements, for example, "we are healthy when we eat *our* food" often proceeded the naming of individual foods or plants. In the context of the second free list, plant naming began, in several cases, with statements to similar effect, for example, "everything, all of the plant, is important for Maya people, for our food, to make our life." This explicit contextualization of the lists, together with the frequencies shown here, support a strong connection between ecological heritage and ideas about what makes a healthy Maya person.

The items listed frequently evoke those that have been important in the past but continue to be utilized in the present, in a process that I argue are a way of constructing heritage. The desire for traditionally grown corn and bush foods, and the framing of this desire in terms of what "the body wants" or what "Indian bodies need," very explicitly draws on heritage ideals as being important when considering healthy food choice. There is anecdotal evidence to suggest that there is a relatively recent increase in these references. The connection between heritage foods, land practices, and recent politics is explored in more detail in the next section.

IT'S GOOD FOR LIFE: TRADITIONAL KNOWLEDGE

"Maya people are stopping their tradition. Indians have to show respect to show they are still Indian." Vernancio had relayed his free list of what makes a healthy person and, although he did not list tradition, he had made the segue quickly after relaying a story about his daughter getting sick one year when he did not grow corn. He was working out of the village and his family ate only rice and flour bought with his wages. He recognized his error and was quick to criticize the movement away from being "Maya." Having spent time working out of the village, his criticisms came with knowledge. He had witnessed Maya men, working alongside Belizeans of many ethnic descents; develop preferences for foods, language, and fashion that were more Belizean than Maya. While the negotiation of a combined Belizean Maya identity is skillfully accomplished by community members, Vernancio's criticism was focused at the heart of being Maya: growing corn to feed your family. Recognizing the importance of this quintessential Maya tradition, and passing it on, in his view, was crucial for wellness.

"The most important tradition is the land. I [am] used to this land. We have to teach children the correct way for our life. When we are a baby, we eat *käla, tutu*—it's not like chemicals. We never had stomach ache because our parents serve us with the best food, no chemicals." Hearing this from Julio did not surprise me. His family often invited me to their home to try traditional foods and learn traditional preparations for harvested or gathered wild foods. His family's home gardens extended far beyond the sight of his house and gave way to the bush, and they further blurred the lines between wild and cultivated by planting wild fruit trees and other bush plants close to the house for easy harvesting. One of the reasons for this serves as a salient illustration of how traditional foods are valued and how this value changes and fluxes. Julio's partner, Florentina, harvests and processes many traditional foods, *ch'i kaay* flower buds and *k'uxub'* (achiote) as examples, for sale in the market in Punta Gorda. The people buying these products are Maya who are either living or working in town, or from villages where people do not have access to land in the same way as those living in Santa Cruz. The demand for these products, by all accounts, is high. People want their traditional foods and they want them to be local, fresh, and plentiful. There is a sense that the increase in desire for these "Maya foods" can be explained, at least partially, by a convergence of factors.

The importance of the land, and traditional forest products and cultivars, to Maya livelihood and identity has been not only recognized but also clearly articulated by academics (Wilk 2007; Grandia 2007; Wainwright 2007) and local activists within the past eight years. This articulation was made in direct support of Maya land claims made in the Belizean high court, the details of which were discussed in the previous chapter. A clear argument can be made that the fight for land rights and traditional land use has drawn everyday gathering and cultivating practices into sharp focus. They have become practices to highlight, to appreciate, to teach, and to celebrate. This contrasts with behavior sometimes observed and frequently discussed in relation to younger generations, particularly with the increase of formal education, distancing themselves from their indigenous traditions. "My children don't like it," Felicitas, Santa Cruz mother of 13, explains. She is talking about *chaiyuk*, a bitter green vegetable similar to spinach found growing wild in the chopped bush and valued by older community members as a "healthy food." Despite the pressures of youth, pride in and desire for traditional foods seems to have been cultivated through the open discussion surrounding Maya identity and the explicit connection to the land. Food is tangible Maya heritage.

I speculated that there was another, relatively new, force that was adding to the positive perception and increased desire for traditional foods. Reginaldo clearly articulated this force after giving his free list of items that make a person healthy. He explained, "those kinds of things—*tutu* (jute), *käla* (jippy jappy), *chaiyuk*—are very healthy for us because you doesn't have to use lard or sugar . . . even nurse and doctor say it." With the 2009 opening of the health clinic four miles away in San Antonio, there has been increased exposure in Santa Cruz to nurses and doctors and the messages passed through these formal health care channels. As evidenced by Reginaldo's comment, as well as those of many others in the village, including Eluterio's rejection of the white chicken, the clinic staff had regularly referred to many traditional foods as healthy foods. Current nutritional science was giving sanction to traditional nutrition.

"We raise everything how we been taught, raise chickens, do *milpa*, ground food, chopping, we eat tortilla so we have to plant corn." As Reginaldo continued to explain how health is related to the foods his family eats, he explained how what they eat is related to tradition. Planting corn is a heritage practice and it is done because corn tortillas are what Maya people eat. In this sense, identity politics, nutritional rhetoric, and other forces that represent "the effects of . . . the power relations imbued in defining 'healthy' food are naturalized" (McMullin 2009: 122).

I argue, then, that there is not one distinct way in which healthy foods become heritage foods. Foods can be considered heritage through their connection to the land and traditional land practices. They become heritage because these practices are embedded in daily life and embodied as part of daily routines. Heritage is constructed in these ways, I argue, without it necessarily being referred to in this way. In part, because of

this, heritage classifications surrounding foods and ecological relationships do not follow one particular cognitive blueprint. The following
section briefly illuminates the development of ways of thinking about
how traditional knowledge is classified, further demonstrating the argument for the firm phenomenological grounding in the measurement and
consideration of how people classify and construct their world.

MORE THAN YOU THINK: RELEVANT HISTORIES

A brief history of Maya cognitive studies shows methodological flaws.
The hot/cold classification system, which was their hallmark, essentially
became a reified form of scientism—forcing informants to select one or
another quality (Tedlock 1987) and leaving little room for variation or
detailed explanation. Long lists of substances identified as having one
quality or the other were collected and published without initial sugges-
tion that adherence to a strict dichotomous structure might be an overly
simplistic way to understand how balance and health were achieved
among the Maya. For example, and of interest in light of the data presented in this chapter, critics found that tortillas, which occupy a primary
position in both the nutritional and the ideological aspects of Maya life,
are neither hot nor cold but neutral. This recognition has led to an equa-
tion of the neutral category with a conception of something nourishing or
healthy. Neutral values help housewives prepare a balanced meal, where
the desired end result is neutrality (Mathews 1983), and may relieve the
pressure to find other foods to feed the family along with tortillas. As
Eluterio's story at the beginning of this chapter demonstrates, tortillas are
healthy, nourishing, and complete.

It has been argued that evidence for balance ideology in the realm of
health was not an elaborate symbolic manifestation of an all-pervasive
system. Rather, health choices were simply pragmatic—the result of test-
ing plants and foods and taking note of what worked to relieve a particular ailment (Baines 2008). Choices became part of a system not because
they reflected particular cognitive structures but because they were of
practical use in a particular environment. Contemporary medical terminology contains "ecological realities" (Hsu 2007: 92) that have become
symbolic languages over the course of complex historical processes,
which relate directly to ecological knowledge is a useful perspective regardless of whether or not "a human propensity for correlative thinking
can be demonstrated by neurobiology" (Hsu 2007: 92). Indeed, Kapferer
(1988) notes that, "no tradition is constructed or invented and discontinu-
ous with history . . . they make sense and condense a logic of ideas which
may also be integrated to the people who make the selection although
hidden from their reflective consciousness." Cognitive systems and lived

experience are interwoven to create a well person. In this sense, food heritage is embodied through daily practice.

The data and discussion related to food and food heritage in the context of the research questions presented in this chapter warrants a consideration of the roots of ways of thinking about cognitive classificatory systems, particularly as they relate to traditional ecological knowledge (TEK). In this study, I ask: is environmental knowledge related to the way the body is conceptualized and how that knowledge is related to the formation of heritage conceptions? Much of the current interest and research associated with TEK reflects a traditional ethnoscientific endeavor of exploring how local ecologies are understood, conceptualized, and categorized by the people that live them (Lauer and Aswani 2009). Indeed, despite the forthcoming critique, the development of TEK as a nexus of consideration, both within and beyond anthropology, owes an ongoing debt to the theory, aims, and methods associated with ethnoscientific pursuits.

The primary theoretical underpinning of ethnoscience is that culture exists in the minds of the informants (D'Andrade 1995:1). By systematically attempting to discover these cognitive systems, ethnoscience introduced both "methodological rigor" and "theoretical depth" in terms of how knowledge was catalogued and, later, disseminated academically (Nazarea 1999). Ethnoscientists, however, "approached their subject with Cartesian assumptions about the relationship between mind and body [and] this perspective continues to guide many indigenous knowledge studies today" (Lauer and Aswani 2009). There is an irony in the recognition of "traditional" social practice and this attempt to highlight and validate these classificatory systems. It can be argued, despite best intentions to elucidate unfamiliar cultural practices and understand them on their own terms, the ethnoscientific approach has actually served to reinforce the superiority of Western scientific practice but illustrating that other knowledge systems exist outside an empirical, ecological reality (Baines 2008).

This critique of ethnoscience, ultimately, is rooted in its fundamental assumptions. "Biological life-forms are not likely grounded in genetically fixed neurophysiological organization" (Randall and Hunn 1984). Indeed, dealing with infinite variable phenomena with a finite set of named and ordered classes leads to data that may or may not reflect the reality of the informants (Baines 2008). The principles of classification are, therefore, arbitrary (Ingold 2000). While Ingold's critique of cognitive classification seems dismissive, it can be argued that, armed with this understanding that cataloguing ethnobotanical information, for example, in this way is not necessarily going to lead to a grand illumination of a complete classificatory framework for a particular community or group, looking to identify the flexing categories, or the processes by which they flex, can be a helpful endeavor. This "sensitivity to context" (Ingold 2000:

161) is what cognitive systems lack. Classification and systemic cataloging are not always the most illuminating pursuits. This recognition drives
this study's phenomenological focus.

Drawing from cognitive aspects of generalized ethnoscientific
thought, Berlin et al. (1973) and others came to represent the intellectual-
ist school of ethnobiological thought. Intellectualism was situated firmly
within anthropology in that it implicitly traced its roots to Levi-Straus-
sian structuralism. Discovering the structures inside the mind that
guided the indigenous classification systems was an objective that allowed little room for discussion of the utility or practical aspects of the
system construction. Taking ethnobiological ideas in a more nuanced direction, anthropologists began to explicitly address the observation that
classification is impacted by human experience in ways that are both
significant and interesting (Hunn 1982). These scholars, led by Hunn, and
including Morris (1984) and Randall (1987), find their intellectual roots in
a functionalist perspective, focusing on the classification of living things
in TEK systems being inextricably linked to their practical functions and
overall utility. "Systems of folk classification, rather than objective recognition of natural patterns, are thought to develop from the unique history
and culturally defined beliefs, behaviors and preferences of a particular
group" (Lampman 2012).

This chapter offers this critique while recognizing the benefits of these
methodological and theoretical roots. The convergence of the intellectual-
ist and utilitarian positions asks how categories and uses are related. The
next section, beginning to address this critique, explores these intersections in more depth, looking toward identifying a community consensus
about what constitutes a healthy life for the individuals of Santa Cruz
through the identification of flexible categories and correlations.

IT KEEPS US HEALTHY: CONNECTIONS AND INTERPRETATIONS

Health and wellness connections to heritage foods and activities were
further explored using both unconstrained (or "free") and constrained
pile sorting techniques. From the two sets of free lists (n = 50, n = 19)
collected, the most frequent responses were written on index cards and,
with the assistance of Basilio and other community members, translated
into Mopan. Additional cards were added and translated representing
feelings associated with wellness/lack of wellness. Foods and activities
that had proven ethnographically salient as either unhealthy or important for life but had not been highlighted with the free listing process
were also added for a total of 55 items. The pile sorts items represented
by an extended domain of wellness, which was designed to explore how
different foods and activities were considered in relation to being well.
This wellness domain drew from two less nebulous domains: foods and

activities (from free list frequencies with "non-healthy" terms added) and emotions and descriptors. Corn, for example, was free listed as something healthy in the first subdomain, while sugar was not but included to represent a potential "non-healthy" term that was ethnographically salient. Activities, working together as an example, were taken from free lists with the "non-healthy" term, fighting for example, was included. Healthy, pretty, satisfied, happy are all examples of emotions and descriptors included, with "hot" and "cold" included as a way of potential getting at humoral classifiers that I determined to be of possible importance.

Pile Sorts, Unconstrained

Requesting respondents (n = 24) sort the 55 cards representing the important foods, plants, activities, and emotions related to wellness proved to be a fruitful endeavor in many respects. First, participation in the exercise was the first time many people had seen certain words written in Mopan. Some had never seen a Mopan word written down at all. Except for a few elders, most of the residents of Santa Cruz are able to read Basic English and, with both languages written on the cards, were able to phonetically read the Mopan, and to correct my spelling, which was taken from the "official" orthography from Guatemala. I was told with frequency, "they don't do it right over there." Most participants seemed pleased to see so many of their important daily items written in their language and were happy to take the time to look through the cards carefully.

The actual request to place the cards in piles of their choosing was taken in stride by a minority of participants and met with some difficulty by most. With the exception of the much older people, who were less likely to read well and more likely to be tired, the sort seemed to be an equal opportunity confounder. After convincing that there was no correct answer, all went on to sort. There was a wide range of approaches to the sort, from narratives constructed from groups of cards, to pair matching, to opposite identifying, to groupings of foods, plants, and feelings. Origins of foods were a popular classifier, for example, "foods that come from the ground" or "foods that come from the tree." "Good to eat," *"kich'pan hanal"* or "good to eat and healthy" were also common. Other approaches included sorting by casual relationships, for example, "you are strong because you take medicine" or "when you work together, you have friends and you are happy. Narrative sorts took these a step further, for example, "you are sad if you are sick but when you get better you can work hard." Notes made during the sorts reveal a wide range of ways of thinking about the domains of health and important knowledge/practice for life.

In order to gain further insight, sort results were entered into AN-THROPAC 4 (Borgatti 1996) for analysis. This DOS-based program calculates the aggregate proximity matrices between responses and represents these data in a two-dimensional plot. This is done through the use of nonmetric multidimensional scaling (MDS), chosen here "due to its reliability as a means of analyzing and representing conceptual information" (Cooper 2009: 137). The limitations of plotting a multidimensional data relationship using just two dimensions are notable and interpretation of the MDS plot proceeds with this knowledge. The acceptable degree of fit is assessed with Kruskal's stress function, with the acceptable stress value at 0.15 or lower (Borgatti 1996). The stress value for the plot shown (figure 3.1) is 0.12, falling within acceptable limits. This noted, all MDS plots are open to interpretation and much of this is done with the benefit of ethnographic data. To enhance clarity, the coordinates were exported to SPSS 20.0 to generate a scatterplot.

In light of the ethnographic data and the research questions concerning health and wellness conceptions and their relationship to ecological practice and experience, the MDS plot shows several points of interest:

- "Healthy" appears in a central location. It is contrasted with sick to its left, along the horizontal axis. Vertically, it is in close proximity to "pretty," which confirms their similarity in meaning as discussed at length earlier in this chapter. To the right along the horizontal

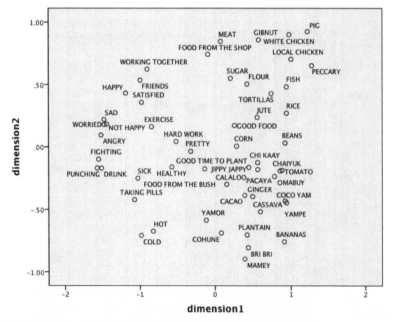

Figure 3.1 Multiple Dimension Scaling Plot: Proximity to Healthy

axis, "good time to plant" is in closest proximity indicating the central of planting knowledge and its importance as healthy knowledge.

- A "healthy" cluster emerges to the left-upper diagonal the "healthy/pretty" area showing an aggregate of "working together," "happy," and "satisfied," along with "exercise" to the bottom, indicating the importance of shared labor to well-being, discussed at length in the following chapter.

- "Food from the shop" forms a straightforward cluster at the top right. "Sugar" and "flour" are part of that. Even though sugarcane is traditionally grown in small quantities and made in the village, most families currently buy it at the shop. "Tortillas" are never bought at the shop but form a close relationship with "flour" — with flour tortillas replacing corn tortillas as the staple at some meals. "White chicken" is also bought at the shop and while it appears near the top as well, it was most commonly sorted with local chicken in the "chicken" or "meat" pile. Interestingly, white chicken is displayed the furthest from "healthy" as possible on the plot, reflecting its frequent use as an example of "unhealthy" food as exemplified in the opening vignette.

- "Good food" and dietary staples form a cluster to the right of "healthy," with "food from the bush" in close proximity toward the bottom and including both wild and cultivated plants, plantains, as examples. This illustrates the blurring of the "bush food" category to include food cultivated in the bush and considered to be as healthy as wild bush foods. The appearance of the bananas and tubers in this category is consistent with the perception of these cultivars as healthy bush foods, or "ground food." The position of calaloo, another semi-cultivated plant, which takes on the status of "bush food," also reflects this blurring.

- The cluster on the left shows a clear association between drinking alcohol to excess and unwellness, with its close proximity to fighting, anger, sadness, worry, and sick. This relationship was reflected ethnographically with alcohol almost always considered to offer a negative contribution to wellness, which is in turn linked to worry and sadness. Men spending family money on alcohol was a worry expressed by many women in Santa Cruz and surrounding villages. The only observations and reports of physical violence that I noted involved the use of alcohol. While alcohol was observed to be used in more moderate and non-violent circumstances, these were never reported nor publicly discussed. It is relevant to note that the perceived problem of drinking leads some families to join Baptist and other Evangelical churches, which do not allow alcohol consumption.

Pile Sorts, Constrained Selections

While the unconstrained sorts provided broad ways of looking at domains of healthy foods and activities, I questioned their utility in providing domain-specific consensus toward the design of a community-driven
assessment of wellness and engagement in traditional ecological activities. With this goal in mind, 30 additional respondents were selected and
asked to complete two directed sort activities with the same 55 cards.
They were asked to select the 10 cards most important to be healthy and,
after replacing those cards, were then asked to select the 10 cards most
important for a "good life." The second question was clarified, in Mopan,
to include both practices and items that one should know about/how to
use to have a good life in the village, essentially to be a "good Maya
person." Respondents were asked, after the sorts, if they felt that anything had been left out or they had wanted to include an item that they
did not find in the cards. Both constrained sorts supported the importance of traditional foods to both health and a good life (figures 3.2 and
3.3).

Unlike previous lists and sorts in which corn did not feature as promi-
nently as might be expected,[7] the constrained sorts were able to confirm
the importance of corn and corn tortillas to health and daily life. Bush
foods were selected frequently, with jippy jappa palm being the most
important wild plant, high on both frequency lists. Other staples ranked
high on the list, with ground foods and bananas again being strongly
linked to health. The overlap in wild food and cultivars linked as healthy
bush foods found in the unconstrained MDS plot is supported by these
results. This is an important indicator of the importance of considering
the practice of planting cultivated foods in the "bush" as a healthy activity. Rather than simply considering foods, plants, or activities as isolated
units, the sort results give weight to the argument that these must be
considered in consort. Without the interaction with the land, planting the
bananas and ground foods in the bush, they would not reach "bush food"
status and perhaps not reach "healthy" status as a consequence. This
relationship between practice and becoming heritage is illustrated as a
phenomenological processing loop in Figure 3.4. This discourse, which
conflates wild and cultivated species and assigns heritage value through
"bush food" status to foods that may be more recent cultivars, is one that
emerged from much conversation with community members throughout
the data collection process. Another example of a cultivated food, which
has taken on "healthy bush food" status in this way, is a leafy green
called calaloo. A cultivated food not unique to Maya communities but
grown and eaten throughout the Caribbean, calaloo has come to be considered an important, healthy bush food.

In the healthy sort, 42 of the 55 items were chosen at least once. Forty
percent (17 items of the 42 total) of the items were chosen by at least nine

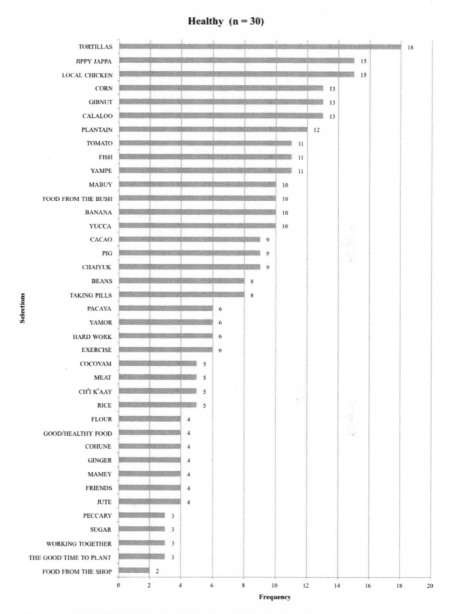

Figure 3.2 Constrained Pile Sort Selection Frequencies: Healthy

of the 30 respondents. In the important to know/use for life sort, 41 of the 55 items were chosen at least once. Thirty-four percent (14 items of the total 41) of the items were chosen by at least nine of the 30 respondents. These percentages reflect a high degree of agreement in responses. The frequencies from the two constrained activities were compared and those

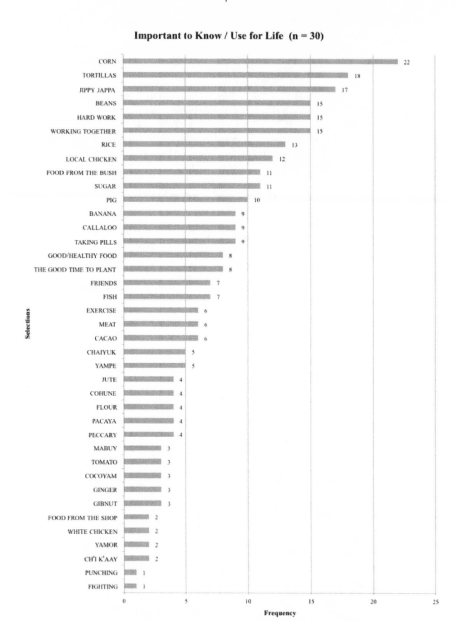

Important to Know / Use for Life (n = 30)

Figure 3.3 Constrained Pile Sort Frequency Selections: Important to Know/Use For Life

items receiving high numbers on both lists were noted. These notes and the frequencies were then analyzed in light of the ethnographic data to determine the topics for 22 questions that were written to form the envi-

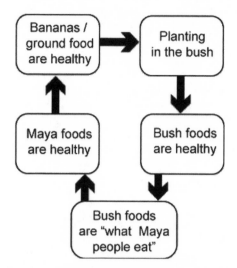

Figure 3.4 Phenomenological Processing Loop: Bananas as a Healthy Bush Food

ronmental heritage and wellness assessment, the design and results of which are presented and discussed in chapter 6.

COGNITIVE PHENOMENOLOGY IS NOT AN OXYMORON: HOLISTIC PERSPECTIVES

The bush food discussion did not end with the blurring of the classification and their identification as healthy foods. Talking about foods from the bush brought references to seasonality and time, and with those new insights into how these temporal ideas intersected with wellness. There seemed to exist a kind of mysterious reverence around bush foods, perhaps a combination of their heritage value and the knowledge and/or skill required to properly harvest them. As discussed earlier in this chapter, a positive perception surrounding the value of these foods exists, in Santa Cruz however; this acknowledgement was met with qualifiers.

"Do you like to use foods from the bush?" I was asking this question to discover more about the perception of these "heritage foods," curious if it was possible for people to recognize the heritage value but not to actually enjoy the preparation or consuming of the foods. I suspected there were nuances behind who did and did not go to the high bush for food.

"Yes," I was told, but "those are from the seasons though." It was not possible to just go to the bush and get whatever food you want like you might at the shop. Later, I revisited the question and another gentleman explained further.

"You can find like that when the moon done get up," he told me about bush foods, referencing the harvesting of the popular jippy jappa palm, which harvested by selective pruning of its young shoot at the waxing to full moon only. Cohune palm leaves, used to thatch houses, are also harvested with care given to the phase of the moon. I experienced first-hand what happens when these temporal conventions are ignored when the roof of the project house was thatched under time pressure and the leaves were cut at the incorrect time. Small worms rained from the roof for many days, calling to mind the biblical explanations for ecological phenomena I had read about as a child.

The measurement of time is, in many ways connected to the seasonality of bush foods. Asking about the availability of certain items or the time for certain events, responses such as "only during the time when there is *ch'ib* (pacaya)" were not uncommon. While activities were marked by seasonal availability of bush foods, so too were foods eaten highly seasonal. Corn, in some form, is eaten every day throughout the year, however, the new harvest, or "green corn" is celebrated throughout the village and the air becomes heavy with gossip about who has the green corn first. Other foods vary significantly throughout the year and are very seasonal. *Ch'ib* is in April, *ch'i kaay* in August, *mabuy* in October. Calaloo and lau grow after the *k'ux* planting, which happens in May. I was beginning to grow used to the anticipation of the next bush food I would have the opportunity to try. There was expectation and anticipation that buzzed through the village. When, in post pile sort conversation about health, teenage sisters told me that it was important to have a "diet to match your body," I thought for a moment they we espousing an exported new age diet philosophy they had learned about at high school. After further investigation, I realized they were talking about seasonal and local food choices. Indian bodies were used to certain bush foods at certain times of the year and of course, as discussed earlier in this chapter, corn.

References to seasonality reflect a sensitivity to ecological factors that have long been a talking point among scholars conducting research revolving about the ways food and eating are related to environmental nuances and wellness in Maya communities (Tedlock 1987; Currier 1966; Anderson 2012). In these studies, temperature, and temperature classifications, play a role in health. This chapter has offered a critique of environmental classificatory systems in general, however, my initial observations in Santa Cruz led me to believe that the documented Maya humoral system of classifying elements of the natural environment; foods and plants, most commonly, might exist in some form. For this reason, I added traditional classificatory categories "hot" and "cold" to the pile sorts, hoping to gain insights into a dichotomous cognitive classificatory system. However, the hot/cold system did not emerge from the data. While temperature was clearly a factor in food/illness relationships, I was never able to tease out more than ethnographic anecdotes about what foods and drink should be given or avoided because of their heat or coolness.

Older women commonly told me about using black pepper "to get the body not to feel pain." Pepper, garlic, and oregano are "hot" and "strong." When these are used, "our body will get strong." Illness or weakness was commonly explained by an ignorance of temperature, or a lack of care to balance the actual temperature (as opposed to a tempera-ture "label"). Understanding of environmental factors, the weather, for example, is crucial. "When the rain start on us, when we are hot, that's how we become sick" my friend told me one afternoon. He was not alone in his understanding of the importance of this etiology.

Both seasonality and temperature speak to rich academic history and debate regarding Maya cognition, practice, and phenomenological expe-rience surrounding the topics of food and the environment. This chapter acknowledges this history while offering data to support the use of the "embodied ecological heritage" framework to move beyond the various dueling dichotomous perspectives outlined earlier. While the systematic search for cultural domains—the application of "grammars" or "rules that people carry around in their heads" (Bernard 2011: 239) has been fruitful in this study and the decades of research investigating the con-nection between Maya life and the environment, it must be contextual-ized. In the critique of this scholarly history, I do not simply suggest that knowledge should be uncovered, recorded, or discussed differently. I suggest that the knowledge of seasonality and specific botanical chemis-try that comes with environmental interaction and ecological "sentiency" (Anderson et al. 2005: 16; Ingold 2000: 10) provides significant physiolog-ical impacts on the body that are "real" (Baines 2008). Through the pres-entation of both categorical and practice-related data through the lens of a phenomenological perspective, this discussion has shown that thought and experience need not be mutually exclusive. They converge in the seat of wellness: the body.

The lived experiences of growing, harvesting, collecting, and process-ing food not only influence the way food is considered, or classified, but the actual physical well-being of the practitioners. Thinking about bush foods as healthy because of their connection to the land and their heritage connotations translates into people reporting feeling healthier when they are engaged with these foods. The data and discussion presented in this chapter demonstrate that health and wellness show a varied but clear relationship to ecological knowledge and practice, in general, and to the construction of food heritage specifically. This is shown both cognitively, in terms of how terms were derived and classified in the free-listing and pile-sorting activities, and phenomenologically, in terms of how people experienced these classifications in their daily lives. The link between thinking about, or classifying, foods as healthy and experiencing increased wellness while engaged with these foods is strengthened through an explicit examination of practices associated with their acquisition.

NOTES

1. Obeah is described with varying frequencies as a reason for illness that is sudden or does not respond to standard treatments. It is not unique to Maya communities and is found throughout Belize and the Caribbean. Similar illness explanations exist throughout the world. It is most closely described as a kind of witchcraft or black magic that is inflicted upon a person by another through rituals, often performed at night. The person will then become ill and bush medicine/healing rituals and/or intensive prayer will become necessary to alleviate the illness. In Santa Cruz, there were several cases of obeah that occurred during my stay, however, care should be taken not to overestimate the extent to which it is given as an explanation for illness. It does, however, speak to the importance of social relationships as they relate to illness, with the malintentions of others having the capability to have negative consequences for health via obeah.

2. Approaching a study with a phenomenological component requires additional methodological considerations beyond investigating the degrees of direct causal relationships between the study variables. Lubeck and Alford (in Watts 2006) note that "the open-ended negotiated, self-conscious character of social interaction means that causation is not linear; relations are contingent and subject to continual change." Ethnographic methodologies are well suited for capturing these linkages.

3. Free listing and pile sorting are useful methodologies in many regards, particularly noted for "gathering data in cognitive anthropology" (Weller and Romney 1988 in Bernard 1995: 239). Pile sorting has been found to be useful in revealing shared/differing perceptions with reference to particular connections and correlations (Bernard 1995: 249).

4. The UKAA or Uxb'enk'a K'in Ahaw Association is an independent Belizean non-governmental organization made up of residents of Santa Cruz village with the broad goal of sustainable land management. The PIs of the larger NSF funded project of which I was a part, in addition to local leaders and activists, helped to facilitate the registration and organization of the community-led group in 2007. The executive committee is elected by the members and serves a two-year term.

5. Fifty free list respondents were identified, primarily, through stratified sampling techniques, using gender, age and religion as strata. The sample was comprised of 25 males and 25 females, ages 11 to 67, with the mean age of 36. There were 24 Catholics, 16 Baptists, eight Pentecostal, and two without specified religion, all self-identified. List lengths ranged from one to 11 items, with an average list length of six items.

6. Nineteen respondents, 10 females and nine males, were identified using similar stratified sampling techniques. The sample contained 11 Catholics, five Baptists, two Pentecostals and one no religious affiliation. The age range was 12 to 63 years, with the average age of the respondents at 31 years. Different respondents were chosen for this second list to avoid the association between lists and assumptions that listed plants should be either "healthy" or related to food. Lists ranged in length from two to 27 items, with an average of eight items listed per person. The total number of responses was 150.

7. When I questioned community members about the omission of corn from free lists, it became apparent that corn was considered an obvious choice, a given, and therefore not really necessary to list, especially if I was trying to learn. I, of course, already knew that corn was important and healthy.

FOUR

Bodies at Work, Bodies at Rest: "We Boss Ourselves"

It was an unfamiliar sight. Two middle-aged men and a young woman were making their way up the hill alongside the river. They were dressed in medical scrubs, carried substantial satchels, and their pale-skinned faces were ruddy from the climb in unfamiliar heat and humidity. Reluctant to mind my own business, I excused myself from my visit (fortunately my host was feeling as nosy as I was) and followed. The only person who lived up that hill was called *na'chiin,* or grandmother, by much of the village and Ixna Lola by the rest, although her given name is Florentina. She and her husband lived back there in a two-room home accompanied sometimes by their daughter and much of the time by their grandchildren. She had a new great-granddaughter whom she seemed to take pleasure in.

The visitors arrived at her house and I could tell from my distance that she had not been expecting them. She was blouseless, as was common for older ladies in their homes, wearing only her voluminous skirt, its hem tucked up into its waistband to enable her to get around with a bit more ease. She accepted the group of strangers, as is the Maya way, and they set about their work. I watched for a moment from a distance and then approached along the narrow mud path and inquired about their purpose. They were an American medical team, doctors with students, who had come to offer medical care to the villages. They had been told about Florentina's condition and had left their treatment area in the village community center to come offer her assistance. I chatted with one of the men while I watched the other team members examining her leg. Her knee was swollen, as it had been since I had known her, and she winced as they touched it. They gave her some pills, which had been designed to reduce the swelling and provide relief from the pain she felt. She seemed

55

to take their visit in stride and I could detect no particular enthusiasm or hostility toward the unexpected "help." I told her I would be back to visit in a short while and left with the group.

Walking back to the community center, the group told me that they came to the Toledo District every year, for a week. They spent a few hours in each village but had to leave Santa Cruz after just a couple of hours because they had run out of medicines to distribute. They were going to Rio Blanco National Park to have lunch and a look at the waterfall. Meanwhile, villagers eager for their diagnoses and Ziploc bags of vitamins milled around on the grass in front of the community center.

"Will you come back?" I asked as they hurriedly packed up the rest of the students into the air-conditioned van. They probably would not have the time or supplies to come back, they said. While I considered the few mothers with their baggies of two-week supplies of vitamins and the rest of my friends looking at me for some kind of "gringo translation" for the tease of help that was occurring, I took the opportunity to attempt to extract whatever information that can be gleaned from a few hours in a few villages once a year. A tall doctor from Texas with a kind and gentle manner gave me a few minutes of his time while his colleagues prepared for their escape from the mob of Maya mothers.

"People here work hard so we see a lot of injuries related to work," he was answering my question about what sort of health problems he had noticed in the Toledo villages.

"Things like 'machete elbow' and pain. We see some ladies with issues with their neck vertebrae from carrying their babies on their head. But mostly people are real healthy here. We don't see a lot of high blood pressure and things like that—problems that we see in the States. They get a lot of exercise with their farming." He was eager to share his thoughts so I asked about diabetes, which had been on my mind as I thought about Eluterio.

"Maybe there has been a little more diabetes lately. Maybe it's because they eat a lot of corn."

With that comment, it was time for him to depart. As the van disappeared down the rocky road, I wondered if they would return with a new supply.

"Maybe they will be back next year?" I shrugged as I turned to face the disappointed mothers waiting for my explanation.

"*Ma' inweel* (I don't know)," I offered and most everyone seemed to accept that. Disappointment, especially with medical care, was not foreign to them. As I followed the path back to Ixna Lola's, I gave some more thought to the morning's experience with the medical team. A friend, another researcher in Toledo, had recently told me of a different team he had seen offering acne medication to teenagers who hadn't realized that they had an "acne problem." The countless hours I had spent considering how biomedicine can be simply an extension of colonialism as it acts as a conduit for Western sociopolitical value systems came flooding back to me as I walked. Santa Cruz's residents, no doubt, have been using the biomedical system to their advantage for many years so this recollection was somewhat unexpected.

"*Ma*, Tuli, *ma!*" My brain was, thankfully, diverted quickly from thoughts of Foucault and his passive bodies as my dog attempted to demonstrate her hunting prowess using the piglets belonging to Florentina's neighbors. I continued to chastise her to little avail, providing amusement to the girls washing in the river below. With crisis narrowly averted, I arrived at my destination hoping to find Ixna Lola feeling better from her encounter with the medical folks. I found her washing her clothes, sitting on a flat rock by her "pipe," as everyone called the pvc tubes and faucets providing municipal water outside the majority of homes in the village. The village has a water pump and storage tank and people pay about $4US a month to have a pipe. It was rare to see ladies washing clothes in the pipe, most used the river, but exceptions were made for illness and injury. It would have been impossible for Florentina, in her current state of mobility, to safely make it down the bank to the river.

"How are you feeling?" I asked, hoping to hear that she felt some relief.

"The same. I have pain. I don't know what I will do. I can't work." I sat with her as she slowly washed each piece of clothing. Everyday tasks were an incredible effort because of her pain. Her knees had been swollen and painful for years now, although there seemed to be an increase recently. She had tried various treatments with varying success but no relief was permanent. Her concern about her ability to work was evident throughout our conversations.

"Sometimes now we don't have any tortillas because I can't walk to the corn mill and my husband, he's old too, but he has to go to the farm." Her living situation was slightly unusual and particularly hard. Her daughter was a widow and had come back to live with her, bringing her children. While this situation may have seemed advantageous, it was currently difficult. The daughter was working for wages in town, coming home only on the weekends. The grandchildren were all in high school. This meant that, during the week, there was nobody at home to help with the work. There were no girls to take the corn to the corn mill and no boys to help their grandfather bring corn from the farm. With everyone at work or school, Florentina was essentially a prisoner in her home, unable to move through the village and surrounding lands to accomplish the work she had done her whole life. Clearly, it troubled her on many levels.

"When you work, you will find good food, that will make you healthy. Not sweating, that is when the laziness comes in your body. When someone is sick, they will not find healthy food." She described the kind of paradox she and her aging husband found themselves in: unable to work because of their sicknesses but unable to get better because of their inability to work (figure 4.1). If she couldn't even make it down the hill to grind her corn for tortillas in the morning, how would she ever get well?

"Santa Cruz is rich with healthy food—ground food,[1] cohune cabbage, jute, *chaiyuk*, calaloo," she explained. You just had to be willing and able to work, to get to the bush and find it and bring it home. She did not have this kind of food very often because of her husband's limited energy but she knew it well, having lived deep in the high bush, several hours walk from the road, for many years of her adult life. She had a unique perspective. Although I had spoken with several village elders who had spent years living in the bush, she had been born and educated in San Antonio, the largest Mopan village and the most "developed" in terms of the amenities offered. She had experienced, in a sense, the two extremes of Maya life in Mopan communities in Toledo as it relates to interaction with the landscape.

"From before when we were living in the bush, we eat all of those things. I could work good then, not like this." Every 30 seconds or so, she turned to her side and spit: a side effect of a treatment she was given a while ago, she says. She is still washing when her granddaughters return from the river with their clean clothes, looking *kich'pan*. I wonder if they ever take their grandmother's clothes and then I recognize the importance of her being able to do at least one of the many tasks she has been doing her whole life. She has just reminded me that when you work, you will be healthy. It is a connection that seems clearly illustrated throughout Santa Cruz but one that seems unfair as I watch a grandmother in pain struggle with each skirt and blouse.

When I checked back with Florentina the following week, she reported that the pills given to her by the medical team had not helped, although she had taken them all. She thought maybe she should try to get

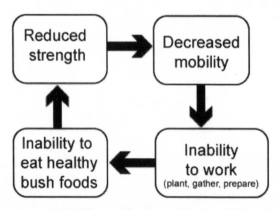

Figure 4.1 Phenomenological Processing Loop: Work and Strength

an injection but was not hopeful about her chances of making it down the hill to catch the bus to get to the clinic. I began to notice other ladies at gatherings sending their children up the hill with food for her and her husband, and there was talk of her grandchildren reorganizing to see if someone could be home with her during the day. She continued to work as best she could for about two years after this day. And then she passed away.

Work cannot be separated from wellness in Santa Cruz. Rather than isolated activities related to acquiring money or resources, work consumes much of daily life in the village. Work is what people do. This is not to say that people do not rest or enjoy themselves; there is much of that. Work, however, forms the backbone of healthy social life and individual well-being. Florentina's story illustrates this. This chapter explores the relationship between work and wellness through an examination of what people do in Santa Cruz, especially as these activities relate to an interaction with the land. I examine this intersection from multiple angles. First, I consider the activities involved in what are considered traditional labor practices and discuss the importance of these activities to the embodiment of wellness. The everyday sensory experience of participation in traditional activities associated with work, I argue, is integral to being well. Next, through and examination of illness reports from two distinct data sets (self-reports and spot observation collected over a period of 10 months), I discuss how being ill affects what people do in terms of their daily work. These data are brought to bear on a discussion of how work activities, or skills, are learned in Maya communities, making an argument for the utility of the embodied ecological heritage framework in the conception of work/wellness relationships.

WE HELP OURSELVES: RECIPROCITY AND RITUAL

"We help ourselves, we help each other. That's how we do it." I was thick into the rigors of the *k'ux* planting season and had fully embodied the tradition of reciprocal labor. I understood what he was saying with my body and my mind. The making of thousands of tortillas had broken through my Cartesian barriers and I heard him clearly. I had been assisting the ladies of the village in baking and preparing meals that accompanied this, the most important planting of the year. My motivation was twofold. I wanted to understand and fully appreciate the value of and obligations associated with the community's system of reciprocal labor exchange. I also wanted to help all the families that had helped me. Their generosity in terms of time, information and, of course, food had been overwhelming and when I was hailed to bake for them, I happily obliged, understanding that this was only a small measure of what I owed them. Limited only by my inability to be in two locations at one time, I pro-

ceeded to bake for as many ladies as possible and eat more pig than I had
ever considered plausible.

Friends and family members helped each other with tasks often, however, during certain important activities, "helping each other" was a far
more structured and crucial activity than this English explanation most
frequently offered suggested. Reciprocal labor exchange, or *usk'inak'in*
(translated loosely "a day for a day") occurs at times when a large number of men are needed to accomplish a large task. Tasks in which labor
exchange will be employed most often include: chopping bush to clear
for planting, planting (corn or rice, sometimes other crops), and building
or thatching houses. Sometimes it will be used for harvesting or building
ranchos (small field houses for corn) but many people prefer to do these
things alone or with a few friends or family. Friends and family are often
involved in more formal labor exchange relationships but large plantings
and house buildings will often require up to 20 men, necessitating the
requesting of services from those outside the family. The nuances of who
is selected are different from man to man and task to task. First, there are
men who owe a day of labor: men you have already given a day to and
they need to "return back the day." Many men will call in the days that
they are owed before requesting labor that they know they will then need
to return. Other factors that I was told can affect the decisions include: if
the men are good workers, if they understand how you like to plant
(sometimes this means if they are in the same family, belong to the same
religion or political party, or from the same place) and if they are available. Every man plants during a 6-week period in May/June so labor can
become scarce, with obligations being made and fulfilled in various locations on any given day. Occasionally, men who owe money to the family
are requested to give a day of work. While this traditional labor system
operates in lieu of the "payment for work" system, everyone is aware of
the value of a day's labor ($10–$20US), and this may be used to settle
outstanding debts. I observed cases where a man had borrowed a sum of
cash from another and then found himself unable to pay the cash back.
When harvesttime came, his labor was called to settle his debt. In a very
few cases, men may combine the reciprocal system with wage labor,
hiring some workers for cash and owing a day of labor back to others.
This, in my observation, is done to free labor hours for use in cash cropping or working out of the village. If you return a day to all your workers,
it is difficult to be involved in other activities, especially during chop-
ping/planting seasons. Only a handful of families in Santa Cruz, however, have the resources or the inclination to pay for labor in this way.

Women, as I illustrated with my experience, also take part in labor
exchange with varying degrees of formality. If a husband is involved in
working with another man, there is an expectation that his wife will help
the wife of that man in the preparation of the meals associated with that
task. For example, during the *k'ux* planting, wives would be expected to

arrive in the morning to bake tortillas and assist in the preparation of the meat to feed the men postplanting. As part of the arrangement, the children of the family will also be fed at that meal. Extras, additional to personal leftovers, will be given to the ladies to take home, however, if a woman is not present, her husband will usually only carry his personal leftovers home.

During the *k'ux* planting, the labor involved in the morning planting is not the only work subject to reciprocal exchange of time. If the family plans to kill a pig to feed the workers, as many do if they are able, the work involved and assistance needed begins the previous afternoon sometime between 1 and 3 pm. In my observations, only a small number of men and women will arrive this first afternoon and, oftentimes, these will be the close relatives and friends of the family. Killing and processing a pig is "a lot of work" and both men and women will readily point this out.

Those who are invited to work this first day will likely spend the majority of the 24-hour period in service, with a short window (four to five hours) to sleep. They are rewarded, however, with the richest meals, fortifying them for their hours of work. While work is considered tiring, and I can attest to this firsthand, it is also considered strengthening. This is a particularly salient paradox. The strengthening quality of the work is most obvious in that the labor is in the production of rich food to provide the calories for the intense labor of planting. Additionally, I argue for consideration of a more subtle counterintuitive way in which the work strengthens the workers, promoting their well-being through sleep deprivation and hours of difficult activity: the embodied experience of ritual practice. Collective participation in these activities strengthens bodies through the embodiment of ecological heritage.

Consider the specific sensory experiences associated with the work of the *k'ux* planting (Table 4.1). When a pig is killed for this special occasion, the death squeal resonates around the village. This sound marks the beginning of the ritual meal preparation. The careful cleaning of the hair from the skin using water boiled in the house and brought outside is methodical, culminating in the sight of the bright blood spilling across the pale, smooth skin as the cleaned pig is cut open. The guts are removed and taken to the river for washing. They are heavy, full of partially digested corn, and the smell is, expectedly, strong. Gut washing is lengthy because it is necessary to be meticulous and the odor intensifies as each intestine is cut lengthwise for thorough cleaning. The smell of fresh lime and soap mingles with the odor as the guts, then hands and feet of those washing, are cleaned further. When the guts are brought back to the house for cooking, the preparation of the chicharron is underway, the smell of rich fat wafting through the air from its outdoor spot on a makeshift fire, inspiring passersby to stop and inquire if they can buy a few pieces, and then be sent away because it is not ready, or there is only

Table 4.1.   Division of labor, *k'ux* planting, 24-hour period*

Men	Women
Kill pig	Boil water for pig cleaning
Clean pig	Wash guts in river
Cut skin and meat	Bake tortillas for chicharron
Cook chicharron	Cook guts
Play corn game	Bake tortillas for late night guts meal
Plant corn	Prepare meat/caldo and bake tortillas for postplanting meal
	Divide extra food to take home

* While gender norms are salient in Maya communities, I did observe some gender flexibility in these activities. Boys are sent to wash guts and carry corn to the corn mill if no women are available. Women make chicharron if they are available. I never observed a woman kill a pig or a man make tortillas, although I heard plenty of stories about the latter.

enough for the special few involved in the preparations. While the skins crisp further, someone is sent to the corn mill to prepare the corn for tortillas to accompany it. Heavy buckets of freshly boiled and washed corn strain muscles as the trip is made for grinding. At the mill, the heavy motor is cranked up, drowning out the possibility of conversation for a lengthy ten minutes for such a large amount of corn. On the return of the ground masa, the familiar scent of corn on the *xämäch* follows quickly and, in moments, all hands cradle a piece or two of rich, savory pig skin. Although this satiates, it is not the only meal that evening. The men gather inside as the day darkens and while the ladies prepare the guts carefully, adding the chopped liver and lungs to the thick, spiced broth, they "pass the time."

"Passing the time while the ladies cook" was the most common response given when I asked why the men traditionally played the "corn game." This game, also called *bool* or marbles, is traditionally played on the evening before the *k'ux* planting,[2] and at no other time during the year. A candle is lit in the darkening room and placed at the end of a rectangular patch of floor cleared for this purpose. The bag of corn seed, selected earlier by the man of the house, is placed next to the candle. Incense is lit in a clay burner and placed in the same cluster. Men casually gather around the rectangle and soon teams emerge from each side of the long sides. Corn kernels are carefully lined up in the center, forming one long line on the packed mud floor.

Play starts as one man shakes four specially prepared kernels in his hand and drops them on the floor. The group watches the kernels and shouts out the result. Each kernel has been blackened on one side with soot from the fire. One black side up, three white sides up: "hunkool!" Two and two: "ka' kool!" Three black, one white: "oxkool!" Four black: "quatro!" Four white: "cinco!" The results correspond to the number of moves the man will make with his counter. Every man has four counters and these can be anything he has brought along: beans, twigs, batteries, crayons, cigarettes, etc. They simply need to be identifiable and different from the other players. Play moves from man to man, with each team attempting to capture the counters of the other team. The victors are those that have successfully captured all the counters from every man on the opposing team.

While there are many versions of the corn game ("the eagle" and "marching ants" were two that I became familiar with) varying in length and details, the salient features are the same. It is always played as a team and team members have an opportunity to take a turn for teammates whose counters have been captured. They "help each other." Teamwork is essential to success in the game, however, each player starts with his own counters and plays them himself. The mood during the game is always lighthearted, with laughing, shouting, and friendly teasing being the norm. Men who arrive to play are always fed soon after the game finishes. The meal is typically the rich broth with the insides of the pig, although beans are an acceptable alternative. Women never play the corn game, although younger boys can participate and young girls often sit with their fathers and watch. Women are usually too busy preparing the meal to watch, but the game is not hidden from them in any way and they will often "take a look" as they move about the room, especially as the meal is finished and the game is reaching its culmination.

While the entire game, indeed the entire afternoon and evening as described here, is an acute, and particular, sensory experience, the end of the game and the completion of the meal preparation are an intense convergence for the senses. Visually, the light is low, with only candles lighting the playing area. Men must be hunched over in order to see the kernels during play. Smoke from the burning incense and firehearth are visible in the candlelight. Pain from hunching over the game play, for the men, and the firehearth, for the women, makes them sharply aware of their bodies. The sounds of laughter and shouts of victory are distinct in the quiet village night, so distinct that walking through the village, it is easy to pinpoint who is playing on any given night. The taste of the rich meal, fat and garlic mingling with liver and the varying textures of the pig innards fills the stomach quickly, especially at so late an hour (the meal is served anywhere from 9 pm to 12 am). The smells of the fatty meal mingle with that of the incense and the fresh tortillas to complete the assault on the senses. In the context of sleep deprivation, the senses are heightened and the experience might easily be described as one of ritual transformation (Van Gennep 2004).

Many elements of the ritual practices described here can be linked to success in work and, thus, an increased wellness using the "work equals health" model described earlier in this chapter. The game's focus on teamwork, on helping each other, and picking up the other's slack when they have used up their "lives" reflects the importance of help in getting the planting accomplished successfully. The women's efforts are equally as important, working together is vital for the preparation of such a large animal in the tropics without refrigeration. There are clear connections to health here, for example, attention to proper hygiene and cooking methods is given the utmost care that it warrants. While work/health connections like this are important to recognize, I hope, through the following example, to make a case for the cacophony of sensory experience, the work rituals of planting, described here as having a powerful effect of health and wellness through its evocation of heritage. While all the senses work in consort to provide an embodied experience, I focus here on smell, which, for me, was incredibly powerful over the course of this experience.

Smell has a powerful role in the communicating of emotions and the evoking of experience. Emotional responses to smells have both ethnographic exemplification and a foundation in biological principles. The hypothalamus, the part of the brain linked to feelings and mood, is affected by changes in smells inhaled (Parkin 2007). This physiological link between smell and emotion gives an additional dimension to the body's response to ritual. The transformation of the body through smells experienced in ritual is *actual* in this sense, not simply symbolic or logical. The hippocampus, another related olfactory center in the brain, is linked to memory. Memory, like emotion, is an important factor in the ritual experience. These elements are linked in phenomenological accounts of olfactory experience. Understood in this way, the memory and emotion evoked through the phenomenological experience are physiologically linked to a successful planting practice.

As the men sit close together to play the corn game, bodily odors from the day's work mix with the incense burning next to the corn seed. It is not a coincidence that the same incense traditionally burned on the eve of the *k'ux* planting is also used in traditional healing rituals. In the performance of a healing ritual, individuals become aware of the presence of others through the inhalation of their odors as well as sharing in the experience of smelling something specific, like incense, which is generated from an outside source. In the context of ritual, odors from neighboring individuals might be seen as a generating presence, or an acute awareness of the body at that moment. The smells created by a specific incense, shared by all the participants in a similar way, leads the participants to the next step in the transformative process—liminality. The odor acts as a socially understood marker for the change in body status. These processes occur cyclically over the course of the ritual as the different

odors intermingle, breaking down barriers and serving to "unite participants in the rite" (Classen 1990). Smell not only provides a social marker
of transition from one state to another (sickness to wellness, for example),
but also is able to strengthen the transition by harnessing a collective
energy through a shared sensory experience. In the case of the "corn
game," players move from friendly competitors, transformed into workers who are relied on for a successful planting. They are players in one of
the most important traditions, the sharing of labor, without which nobody would have the corn needed to feed their families. Smell, in this
sense, is both part and a means of spiritual and material transformation
(Parkin 2007: 40). In ritual and in therapeutics, it taps into the physical
responses that keep a body well. I argue here that as people experience
the smells, sights, sounds, and tastes surrounding traditional work practices, they are seen as contributing to keeping bodies well in Santa Cruz.

Traditional practices can be categorized most frequently as work practices as much of daily life in a subsistence farming community, as illustrated earlier, is referred to as "work." Inspired by my immersion in the
work of the *k'ux* planting I asked ten men, middle-aged and older, what
they thought the most important work-related traditions to practice were.
The conversations were open-ended and the men were free to interpret
"important" however they wanted. All of the men mentioned that they
thought the traditions they mentioned were important for young people
to learn and all said they were important for a "good life" or to be
healthy. Table 4.2 summarizes the results of those conversations. Traditional activities that were emphasized by respondents and/or mentioned
by multiple respondents were weighted more heavily and appear closer
to the top of the table.

This list clearly expresses the link between work and ecological heritage practice. For the most part, the practices I observed and participated
in reflect these important traditions. Much of the daily work of women:
washing, cleaning, and cooking, is missing from this list as might be
expected with the male sample; however, baking tortillas, and the processing of corn for the tortillas, remains central to what women do and is
represented here. The movement away from some of these traditions,
particularly the last two listed, is certainly occurring in Santa Cruz. While
the Evangelical religious expressly forbid their members to burn incense,
other younger members of the village just cannot see the point in practicing what they see as something with no foundation in science. "It's not
hurting anything but it's not helping crops grow or anything either" is a
perspective I observed several times. Work practices are changing, too,
albeit in ways that are not as immediately obvious. The next section
explores these changes and trends.

Table 4.2.   Important work traditions, in order of importance (n = 10)

planting/when to plant

rotating fields

working together

playing corn game

building houses

chopping (where, when)

harvesting

baking tortillas

shelling corn in the morning

how to use the plants

rearing animals

burning incense

abstaining from sex during planting times

WORK AND LAND: CONNECTIONS AND DISCONNECTIONS

"We boss ourselves." Filiberto was talking to me while swinging in my hammock. I was sitting by my open door on a small banco, or wooden bench, commonly used in homes in the village. It was the perfect height for baking tortillas but, instead of working, I was looking out into another afternoon rain. Filiberto had been going house to house collecting demographic information for a government assistance program and I was fortunate that the rain had trapped him in an extended conversation with me about work and tradition in Santa Cruz.

"I tell them, 'why do you want to go out? You have everything here. We have our land. You can work and make your farm and you don't have to do what a boss is telling you.'" He continues to tell me about how recent high school graduates talk about getting jobs out of the village. He is clear about the folly he sees in this. Unlike the older men in the village who I have heard criticize a boy when he desires to "go out," Filiberto speaks from a unique insider perspective. At 23, he is not much older than the recent graduates he talks about. Additionally, he is a graduate himself. Excelling in high school, he is frequently offered jobs outside of the village. Some of them, like the job collecting household data that has brought him to my house today, he takes. Others, he would not consider. He clarifies his position on work.

"I can work when I want to work. If I have my farm and I work hard then I have the benefits. If I don't want to work a day, then I make it so I don't work. I work hard but it isn't somebody else that has the benefits." He and I continue to discuss how the expenses of living outside the village are high with rent and buying food. These expenses do not exist in the same way in Santa Cruz, where most food is grown and the land is owned collectively so rent, for houses or property, does not exist.[3] The allure of "going out" or "working out" of the village is tempered by stories told by men who left and then came back. Wages were not enough to warrant giving up the opportunity to make their own farms.

This critique of wage labor in contrast to subsistence farming seems especially powerful coming from someone so young and educated in the national formal education system. He seemed to approach the topic of work not so much from the perspective of the importance of keeping tradition but with a practical and logical rationale. He sounded like a young entrepreneur. Indeed, he seemed to live the "good life." He was recently married and his wife, who was smart, capable, and beautiful, had recently given birth to a healthy baby boy. He, along with his brother, was able to support his grandmother through his skilled farming practices. He worked closely with his uncles and had learned how to successfully plant cash crops as well as the food his family desired. His aunt had told me one afternoon that his wife "could have anything she wants." His farming work still left him time to take short-term jobs outside the village as well as give extensive volunteer hours to the Baptist church. Resting in his hammock and playing with his son were frequent activities I noticed when I visited him at home, or passed by on my way to visit his neighbors.

There seemed to be a certain irony to what he was sharing with me. While the educated teenagers felt the pull away from their farming traditions to enjoy a more "modern" life associated with working in offices, shops, or resorts for wages, Filiberto seemed to be describing a version of the American dream; a recasting of Maya traditional agricultural practice as the product of a self-made man building his own small business and taking care of his family. This discussion was less about Maya bodies needing corn or traditional practices being central to being a healthy Maya person. Ultimately, though, it speaks to a connection to a particular ecology being central to a "good life." The land of Santa Cruz is crucial to the wellness of young entrepreneurs like Filiberto just as it is to the older residents. His opinion about the regrets young people might have if they chose to "go out" was not without foundation.

"[Working] out there, it's lone criminals. When I reach back home, I feel happy." I was talking with a police officer who had spent some time working in Belmopan about wellness. It was clear he had mixed feelings about his decision to leave his village to work. He valued friends, working together, and the more peaceful, quiet life in Santa Cruz, while still seeming to enjoy his job. The quiet life, however, was not for everyone and some young people craved the activity in the towns. They wanted to work out of Santa Cruz because they found the life "too boring." For them, a consideration of the social had to be balanced with economic possibilities.

Ultimately, Filiberto was not alone in his critique of wage labor as a step up on the hierarchy of work. Stress, worry, and the necessity to work for someone else's gain made leaving the village unattractive to many. While work in the village was associated with health, happiness, and prosperity, work out of the village would provide worry and sadness. A happy man bosses himself.

WITHOUT WORK, WE CANNOT LIVE: SICKNESS AND HEALTH/ PERCEPTION AND PRACTICE

As I have demonstrated in this chapter thus far, wellness and work are linked in many ways. Time spent working is linked fundamentally to social expectations and overall well-being. It follows, then, that work time lost to illness will have a significant impact on social well-being, as well as the more obvious economic and nutritional impacts. In order to further investigate how illness is perceived and experienced in Santa Cruz, in addition to what illnesses might pose potential threats to the ability to work, I conducted an illness recall interview with 55 respondents in July of 2010. These respondents were asked to name illness they and the members of their household had experienced in the previous 10 months. They were then invited to discuss the possible reasons for these illnesses, in addition to whether these illnesses had prevented them from accomplishing their work. Thirty-one different responses were given, ranging from the common "fever" (n = 25) to the more obscure "stones" (n = 1) and "bad tongue" (n = 1). Eleven respondents (20%) reported that there was no illness in their household in the past 10 months.

While the collection of the illness recalls proved useful in identifying the types of illnesses experienced most and/or of greatest impact in terms of their likelihood to be remembered and relayed, it revealed little about the impact of illness in terms of loss of time working. I frequently witnessed people continuing to work through relatively minor bouts of fever, colds, and headaches, which were the top three responses. Collecting the recalls on a household level meant that many fevers and colds were attributed to children. While a sick child can mean parental work time lost, the extent of this was difficult to measure. Additionally, while recalls are not uncommon in the ethnographic methodological toolkit, they are criticized alongside other methods that rely on both accurate memory and accurate reporting by respondents (Borgerhoff Mulder et al. 1985). In order to critically address these concerns, I turn to a brief analysis of data collected during my final eight months in Santa Cruz, time allocation spot observations.

While spot observation provides a valuable methodology for uncovering episodes of wellness and illness that could be more valuable than health recall questioning in some ways, I argue that rigorous descriptive ethnographic observation provides this understanding of time conceptions and this is a necessary first step for conducting spot observation. Spot observation techniques should not receive undue reliance and "both interview and participant observation increase our confidence in the validity of the results of systematic observation" (Johnson and Sackett 1998). Using these methodologies in a complementary fashion both work/ wellness spot observations and health recalls, gives the researcher a behavioral and physical measure set against a more phenomenological one, building the holistic picture that I aim for with this study.

Spot observations provide a valuable contribution to the study of practice and how the body moves in its environment. "Behavior refers in phenomenological terms to changes in location, posture, expression and vocalization" (Johnson and Sackett 1998). Physical descriptions are helpful in understanding how behaviors become "habitus" and how this, ultimately changes the physical body in ways that can be significant to health and wellness. Young (1980) demonstrates the social, and to some extent physical, importance of the position of the body in her feminist essay incorporating ball-throwing technique. As Borgerhoff Mulder et al. (1985) point out, the physical descriptions and those related to behavioral consequence allow for different sets of questions, as well as producing distinct, yet relatable, data sets. In general, observing behavior rather than simply focusing on subject reporting aligns with the processual focus of the research presented here and my interest in looking at knowledge and, gaining insight into how connections are made and processes unfold—the "looping" process. Understanding this necessitates a consideration of what people do and not just what they say. The particular advantage offered by these studies is that they offer the ability to differentiate between what is ideology and what is reality through noting what *is* important versus what the informant says is important. This is not to suggest that teasing out the differences between ideology and reality at the intersection of bodily practice is simple. What people think about what they do has a clear effect on what they do; however, this relationship is not necessarily linear in nature. Small changes in thought might be reflected in subtle ways in practice. While spot observation does not always reveal these subtleties, it can provide us with comparative data to continue the discussion.

While increasingly difficult to accomplish as my time in Santa Cruz increased and people came to know me better, the effectiveness of random spot checks in "broadening exposure to local scenes and bringing serendipitous insights" (Johnson and Sackett 1998) was effective and appealing. Although the dangers of being conceived of as behaving erratically were very real, the data collection took me to parts of the village at hours of the day when I would not have normally been there to observe what was taking place. In this sense it "worked" as an ethnographic tool, in addition to providing a wealth of data about how people in Santa Cruz spend their days; types of work, times of rest, and all activities in between are represented in this data set. Among the data, which are to be fully discussed in upcoming publications, are observations related to when people were sick.

While spot observations were recorded for each person over seven years of age in a household, sickness recalls described earlier were collected on the household level. To address this, multiple illnesses observed in one household on one day were counted multiple times only if the illnesses were distinct episodes. For example, if a parent was involved in taking a sick child to the clinic for a fever, both the parent and the child were coded as "S" for sickness/activity related to sickness. These were entered as one fever to reflect the actual numbers of illnesses per household. While this does not perfect the data for comparison with the recalls, it does control for the overreporting observed sickness. The data were compared with the illness recall data and several initial observations were made. First, the prominent illnesses reported, fever, headache, and colds, were also reflected in higher numbers in the observed behavior. Overall numbers, however, were significantly lower. Even accounting for the two-month difference in time of illness,[4] illnesses were reported at higher frequencies and with more diversity than they were observed. Out of the 340 observations, 14 types of illness and 42 total individual illness reports were made, while out of the 55 reports, 32 types of illness and 146 total individual illness reports were made.

There are several possible reasons for this divergence. First, spot observation behaviors are given just one code. For example, if a woman has a headache but is baking tortillas when the observer arrives, she may be coded only as "MP" for "meal preparation" *or* "S" for "sickness" and not both. Although the "sickness" code should take precedence, as an observer, without extended interaction with the woman, I would likely code her behavior as "MP." This is especially true, I would argue, with unfamiliar observers. While Borgerhoff Mulder et al. (1985) argue that unfamiliar observers have an advantage because they record only what they see and do not bring any extraneous knowledge or bias to bear on what they see, this can be less advantageous when recording sickness. If the woman baking tortillas was a friend, she might look up and tell me that she had a headache while she wouldn't share this with a new visitor. When I was out of the village and new researchers were collecting data, no codes of "sickness" were entered for the 50 household observations undertaken. I suspect that some people were experiencing minor illnesses but were engaged in other activities that were more readily observed.

Perhaps this methodological limitation can be addressed through a discussion of what questions are to be addressed with these data. For the work/wellness discussion presented here, I am most interested in sickness that might inhibit the ability to work. An argument could be made that if a woman is baking tortillas with a headache, the headache is not an illness serious enough to consider in this discussion. Indeed, the most reported illnesses differ in not just their higher frequency but in their lack of severity. While the observed illnesses are less frequent overall, those types that were noticed and coded were, with significantly higher ratios, those that affected the ability to work, such as back pain and eye pain. Without the ability to lift or see, much of the daily work in Santa Cruz would be impossible. Indeed, back pain and fever were the two most frequent sicknesses people reported for missing work. While these problems are important to note, it is also important to report that, out of 340 independent observations of household groups, only 35 (10.2%) were observed to have any sickness, however minor. Combining these observations with the self-reports and illness types, it is reasonable to reach the conclusion: the people of Santa Cruz are relatively healthy in terms of work missed.

Recognizing that the villagers of Santa Cruz are, in terms of work missed, healthy does not diminish the observation that being well and able to work is a daily concern. Environmental factors play a strong role in what contributes to being ill or being well (Table 4.3).

Being out in the bush, the farm, or the river is essential to accomplish daily work for life, yet it comes with potential exposure to risk. Not taking care of yourself by becoming trapped in the rain or bathing when your body is too hot was, by far, the most common reason given for minor illnesses, like fresh colds and coughs. Learning to keep yourself dry and well in the natural environment was a skill that was valued, and one that had to be learned through practice as I found out myself. The next section explores ideas about how this learning takes place and how the skills associated with a healthy working life are acquired and reinforced.

SKILLED BODIES, HEALTHY BODIES

"The way they build house is an important tradition—with men, with your family. Now it's changing. The oldest are going. The boys don't know how to tie sticks. Maybe they don't want to try it—they won't learn. If you try it, you will learn. Some girls can't turn on the komal."

This was not the first time Martha had talked to me about tradition and work. She had been raised in a family skeptical of new religions and competing views of what you should or should not practice. In a sense, her views were the most "traditional" in that they reflected what she knew of growing up in Santa Cruz, without the additional behavioral doctrine associated with religious belief tacked on. However, despite her

Table 4.3.   Reasons for (lack of *) illness

bathing while hot/getting wet in rain

working hard/lot of work

being frightened

bike accident

washing far/lot of washing

dropping in creek

have period

dropping in hammock

playing too much

making baskets

bad wind passing

heat of the dirt/dust

pregnant

snakes

don't eat canned food *

God takes care of me *

neighbors' religious beliefs, the learning process that is reflected in the quotation above is the norm in her community. Learning to work well means understanding how to use items from your environment. Using these items means going to retrieve them and after watching someone, usually a parent or grandparent, using them yourself. This process of learning to work by working means that traditions are easily lost if they are not practiced. This is a fear that Martha expressed when she talked about the children not practicing their traditions. She was clearly worried, recognizing that, for her, changing traditions and work practices would lead to laziness and illness. A skilled person is a healthy person.

Learning, popularly associated with the cognitive processes, is, in Belizean Maya communities, expressed in terms of "work" or a body process (Zarger 2002; 2011). If the body essentially "learns" before the mind, the directionality implied in the Cartesian dichotomy becomes muddled and, if we are to fully understand how wellness is conceived and expressed, should be de-emphasized as it has been in this study. The blurring of this distinction is echoed in Izquiero's (2005: 768) observation that the Matsigenka of Peru "do not make a clear distinction in their everyday practices between illnesses and states that affect the body, the mind or their society: emotional, social and physical well-being are all integral parts of what constitutes a healthy life." The semantic gray areas and Cartesian confusion are confounded (or perhaps made moot) in many ethnographic situations in which none of the terms are salient. Many cultures, including, notably, several indigenous groups in Central and South America, do not have a single domain that is coterminous with the notions of "health" or "wellness" (Levin and Browner 2005). However, the intertwined ideological conceptions associated with a healthy body do overlap in some respects with elements identified in holistically focused Western notions, for example, balance, normatively positive behavior and, most important to the discussion in this chapter, the ability to be economically productive. I argue that the learning and practice of traditional work skills in Santa Cruz does not simply enhance subjective well-being through the participation in normative behavior, but wellness in a broader sense, including the physical component, if we insist on the dualism.

Rethinking the way environmental knowledge is learned provides a foundation for understanding how environmental and cultural heritage traditions can be practiced and expressed in individual bodies. Considerations of learning in situ, and its simultaneous effect on the body, owe a debt to Bourdieu (1977) and his articulation of the importance of practice. Habitus, as a theoretical concept, helped pave the way for focusing on the importance of skills. Its recently articulated application in terms of the acquisition of specific ecological skills is exemplified in ways of using the landscape, or "working": clearing and preparing the land for planting, fetching, and preparing wild plants for use or in fishing practice, as examples (Zarger 2011; Vermonden 2009). The ecological body as heritage might be thought of as a way of getting at an intersection of the classic theoretical concepts of habitus and embodiment. Habitus evokes bodily change or learning with the body over time. In this sense, the body can be conceptualized as changing in response to practices that may come to be considered heritage.

While embodiment's theoretical focus on the lived experience of an individual is a useful way of uncovering the nuances of what it means to be healthy, it might be criticized for its internal, individualized focus. Ingold's (2000) "enskillment model describes 'give and take' interaction with their natural environment, incorporating ideas of sensory experience and cognitive patterning as reflections of a greater understanding of how individuals operate in the world. Using his 'processing loop' model, the individual experiences of sensation, touch and taste for example, are indicators provided by the natural environment as to the properties and effectiveness of a food, herb or medicine" (Baines 2011). Equations can be made to the ritual planting activities described earlier in this chapter, however, these experiences do not have to be as acute to be part of the way work becomes related to wellness. Walking to the cornmill every day is an enskilling experience.

The development of skill in terms of work practice is an important way ecological practice is embodied in Santa Cruz. This chapter demonstrated several ways in which this occurs: through ritual sensory experience associated with work practices, through the traditional or heritage practices themselves, and through the ability to be well enough to work. The convergence of these work/wellness intersections addresses the question of how skill specifically is related to both ecological practice and conceptions of heritage. The consideration of skill is taken up in the next chapter as part of a discussion of how education, both informal and formal impacts wellness in Santa Cruz.

NOTES

1. This comment also provides support for the argument made in the previous chapter pertaining to the process by which cultivated ground foods are described as "bush foods" and, consequently, healthy, heritage foods. Note that "Santa Cruz" provides these healthy foods: the land as opposed to the farmers.

2. Although simply a game in the tradition of Parcheesi, it bears an association with traditional ritual elements of the night before planting and is, therefore, exclusively played by Catholics in Santa Cruz. While I discuss this ritual in terms of its importance for the embodiment of traditional ecological practice, it is important to note that non-Catholics in Santa Cruz follow a very similar pattern regarding work associated with the *k'ux* planting and, thus, much of the argument presented here might be applied, at least in part, to those households.

3. It is important to note that while some villages do have portions of collectively owned land, Santa Cruz is one of only two villages in the Toledo district that operates entirely using the collective system of land tenure. Leased land makes many of the decisions and discussions presented here more complex.

4. While two more months of observation would have likely yielded more sickness observations, it seems unlikely that asking respondents to recall eight months as opposed to 10 months would have yielded less reports. Additionally, increasing observations by 20% to reflect the two additional months still has observation frequencies falling significantly below report frequencies.

FIVE

Educating Well:
"They Are Lazy to Learn It Now"

It was not a position I had been in very often, but, nevertheless, it was where I found myself that morning. My digestive system had, for the most part, grown accustomed to the unique micro-organisms of the Toledo district and I needed only to visit my own latrine, and on a relatively regular schedule. For reasons unknown, however, I found myself that morning in the very well-kept latrine belonging to some friends centrally located in the village in the midst of my own illness experience. I sat for a minute pondering the cleanliness and then drew a conclusion, not based on much evidence or prior research, that this must be because the family consisted of only daughters. While I was mentally scolding myself for my judgment of the latrine habits of little boys all over the world, I sought to distract myself from the pain in my abdomen by preparing myself for my exit. Toilet paper is an expensive luxury in Santa Cruz and not one I expected to find. Corncobs are traditionally used but many families use other items as well, usually paper of some sort. My option that morning was a stack of discarded school papers. As I tested the papers for softness, I began to read them.

The two oldest daughters of the family were in high school and very good students. The paper I was holding had received a 20/20: 100%. It consisted of four questions and answers about institutions and, as an example, schools. In the correct answers, an institution was described as serving the "particular needs of society" and having "rewards and punishments." I thought for a moment about learning in this context. My conversations over my many months in Santa Cruz had begun to make me wonder what "particular need" formal education was filling in this particular community. High school in particular seemed to be a source of stress rather than a serving a need. In the next question, the functions of a

75

school were listed: "to be educated, to learn more, to succeed and to make life easier." The third gave the responses to why schools have endured over time: "we need education and we need to live a better life and more easier." I saw the connection between a "better life" and fulfilling particular need but I knew firsthand how difficult it is to define what a "better life" actually was or how life could be made easier.

The last question on the paper asked which rules should exist in every school. I was curious about this answer. Could there really be rules for every school, especially if, by definition, they exist to serve the needs of a particular society? The correct answers given were: 1. You should have equipments. 2. Get permission from teacher before you leave the room. 3. Respect others and belongings. While these seem adequately generalized for the full marks the answer received, I wondered how these might align or conflict with rules of learning and living in Maya society. One, in particular, stuck me as in conflict with the rules of social behavior I had experienced in Maya households. There is a certain level of personal autonomy, which is reflected in a high degree of freedom as far as immediate activity. Even small children do not get permission to leave a room or go outside. Instead, they follow their own needs and wants at the moment.

At that moment I wanted to remove myself from the small wooden house and seek some bush medicine for my still aching stomach. However, that morning in the latrine led me to think about the connections between education and health in several ways. First, I considered the building of latrines in Santa Cruz and how this was a reflection of formalized health education efforts. These efforts, which include many standardized public health directives, for example, washing hands, are supported by the formal school system. Next, I considered how school is represented, in the assignment I read, for example, but also in a wider context, as being essential to well-being in the sense that it promotes success and a "better life." Finally, I considered how school papers have replaced corncobs in some village latrines. This might be interpreted as a telling indictment of how disposable the information found on school papers is considered by many community members. It may also be a metaphor if not a telling indicator of what formal education means for traditional farming practice. It is very difficult to be in school and grow corn at the same time. Young men must choose what they will focus on. It is very difficult to be in school and process and prepare corn at the same time. Young women must choose what they will focus on. This chapter examines these choices as they relate to wellness in Santa Cruz. It presents data from formal interviews with community elders that discuss fears and hopes about what the increasing prominence of formal education will do for overall health and wellness, in general, and traditional knowledge and practice, in particular, in Toledo. In part as a response to these concerns, I discuss my collaborative efforts to address the gap between formal and traditional education, in relation to both information and learning style.

FORMAL EDUCATION IN BELIZE

Atop a small hill just off the main road in the center of Santa Cruz sits the Santa Cruz Roman Catholic School. Like most villages in Toledo, Santa Cruz has just one primary school. Primary school in Belize serves students from ages four to 14, depending on their specific needs and parental desires. Primary schools in Belize offer eight years of instruction, Infant I and Infant II and Standards I through VI. High schools offer an additional four years and are not required. Entrance to high school is determined by exam score on the Primary School Examinations (PSE), taken in the spring when students are in Standard VI. Students must score a 40% or higher to be considered for high school, with certain high schools requiring higher scores. The school system used in Belize has been carried over from the British colonial system, which augmented the basic curriculum brought to the villages primarily by the Catholic Church in the middle of the 20th century. Currently curriculum is managed through the district government education offices and buildings and teachers are managed primarily by the Roman Catholic Schools offices, with a few being managed by the government offices and some through the Methodist Church.

In Santa Cruz, as in many villages, there is a generalized dissatisfaction with the school-based education provided. While principals at village schools have to manage with lack of funding and staff, they also often are faced with problems related to the school buildings; lack of water supply, toilet function issues, bat infestation, and broken/missing furniture are all examples I witnessed firsthand. Parents often complain that teachers do not live in the village and are therefore out of touch and unavailable when it comes to student needs. Teachers often complain that parents are uninvolved and disinterested, always busy with work, and some not having completed their own primary school education. Teachers deal with the added stress of traveling in and out of the community daily and are subject to bus schedules and their unreliability. While parents and teachers both struggle to push for the best for the village children, the results often seem unsatisfactory to both. Though some children manage to excel in this environment, many are considered troublesome, fighting and misbehaving, unable to sit and recite their various times tables or prayers by rote. These primary school conflicts are reflected in the mixed messages children receive as a part of their daily educational experience. While the basic lessons, English and Math as examples, are taught to a high level, other lessons include very little that is of direct use in the daily lives of the students. One morning, as I was concluding some work with the students (described later in this chapter), this disconnection between home life and school life was brought into sharp focus.

As I waited for the children to complete their papers, I glanced up at the health poster hanging above the chalkboard at the front of the class. It was colorful and eye-catching with a river running through the middle. As I read each block of small print, I realized that it was giving health advice and depicting what to do and not to do to stay healthy in your community. Toward the top of the figure, I noticed that bathing and washing clothes and dishes in the river was depicted as something to be avoided. At that moment, about 10 am, I knew that most of the women in the village would be doing just that, washing and bathing in the river. There was an irony that many of these women spent longer hours washing because their daughters, who might otherwise be helping, were sitting in the school classroom, potentially learning opposing lessons.

The formal education system in Belize, as this example in public health education illustrates, has been criticized not only for providing information that is not of great practical use to its students, but also for undermining traditional values and practices. While this is not intended to be an indictment of every classroom, every teacher, or every lesson, it exists as a real source of conflict and stress for both children and parents. Teachers are often caught in the middle and try with their own efforts and funds to supplement the curriculum with relevant local examples. The mainstream curriculum, however, must be mastered and consists largely of information deemed important for all of Belize, from Creole city children to children of Maya subsistence farmers.

The conflicting and unfamiliar advice from school supports the fears of many parents with regard to the school systems. While these fears, discussed in more detail in the next section, are very real for parents, it is important to note that a high value is still placed on formal education. Parents, in general, want to send their children to school. Doing well on exams so that you have the opportunity to go to high school is encouraged and celebrated. Through their frustrations, I noted many parents make considerable sacrifices to send children to high school, indicating the value that it continues to hold in the community.

CLEAN, WHITE SCHOOL SOCKS

"I think that school is the problem. People learn about all these things and they don't want to farm anymore. They want jobs but there are no jobs around here." I was in San Antonio, the neighboring village to Santa Cruz and one which, by all accounts, was "less traditional" or "more modern." The young man who spoke these words admitted he had benefited from a high school education. He had recently married a friend of mine from Santa Cruz, an intelligent young lady who had not gone to high school, choosing instead to help her aging grandmother with her work until she became engaged. I met the couple on the street and the young man had begun a conversation about the growing concern in his large village about idle young men with little to do but "make trouble." I had heard complaints about this problem before and had asked him what he thought the root of it was. While I, as I have already made clear in this chapter, had been presented with much data to suggest that formal schooling may have negative as well as positive repercussions for people living in the villages of Toledo, his speculation as to the reasons for destructive youth behavior was surprising. Familiar with the rhetoric of my educational sphere, which draws the line firmly from more education to less "troublemaking," I wondered about his firm indictment of education as the *cause* of the disruptive behavior. I had heard that school was the death of tradition, which was not an unfamiliar trope to me, but this comment took that trajectory one step further. He made this indictment from an informed perspective: he had been part of the educational system but had returned to San Antonio to farm.

"People talk, talk, talk. They don't do nothing." It was a few weeks later and I was speaking to one of the staff members at a local high school, Tumul K'in Center of Learning, that hopes to integrate traditional Maya heritage knowledge and practice into the standard high school curriculum. He, like the young man mentioned above, was also from San Antonio and was commenting on the increased numbers of idle young men getting into trouble. He went on to explain about the disjunction between school values and Maya values.

"I don't know why they have to use the human rights in our culture. Maya people have their way but when they come out of school now, they don't want to do nothing." He went on to talk about how parents continued to provide food and shelter, even if their children were not working or in school. While children are in school, he explained, they do not learn to do traditional work so when they finish school, they are simply idle. He continued.

"I like how we grow when our parents raise us. You have to get some firewood before you come in, then you can drink. Another bunch, then you can eat. It's good for those people to learn to live because living is not easy." Although Santa Cruz does not experience the same level of "trouble" as San Antonio in terms of violence or drunkenness, these types of fears, and the framing of these fears in terms of a disconnection from traditional Maya land use practices, is common. While elders commenting on the negative aspects of youth practice is not uncommon generally (here and in many places around the world), both informal and formal interviews brought this commentary to the surface quickly. When asked what he would like to see children learning in the future, a Santa Cruz elder gave the following response:

> I would really want to see the young people learn about farming. They
> should learn how to plant, harvest for their own. Today these young
> people are no longer doing so. They go to school. After they complete
> school, they left their village to seek employment somewhere else. So
> today the young people do not want to work on the land. They prefer
> to be career people such as computer tech, police, soldier and secretary.
> These young people look forward to have their own money. On the
> contrary when we were growing up, they teach us the importance of
> working the land. It is a change with the young people today. . . . It is
> important to learn about the way of life, planting seasons, etc. Today
> we the Mayas are losing the value of our culture/tradition.—Susano
> Canti

School is singled out here as the reason that the value in practicing Maya
traditional land use is lost. Other elders expressed similar views, illustrating the preference and disconnection by referencing the land directly.
When asked about young people and the use of traditional medicines,
one elder responded with a scathing remark.

"Some are lazy to go and find it in the bush. They dirty their pants."
The connection between dirt and working the land was also expressed in
reference to the clean, white school socks that the high school children
wear as part of their uniform. These socks seem to have become a symbol
for many people, a visual reminder of who is being educated by working
the land and who prefers the classroom. Not all calls for traditional land
use are as critical in terms of school. The following response to the same
question, "what would you like to see children learning in the future?"
takes a more measured approach:

> The young people should be working on land, to sell so that there is
> food and all would be well. We are rich with land here. We just need to
> work. We should work than to let the land waste. We don't need to buy
> then. The most important skills are to know what to sell and plant.
> School is also very important—it enables you to learn other skills, like
> having easier job. For example; working in the farm is hard—the good
> part is you don't need money when you work. A lot of young people
> are not working. They are moving to another place. They should be
> working in their own community so that they could show that land is
> important to them.—Jose Mes

This response, given by a younger father of six, supports land use and
recognizes its importance not as much for the sake of tradition explicitly
but for the benefits of being able to sell products that are grown. Like
both the high school paper response discussed in the opening of the
chapter and the school staff member discussed earlier in the section, this
response mentions the "ease" of life. Farming is hard work and school
may prepare you for an easier life. How one might test the truth of this is
not easily discovered, however, it is important to note the heritage value
placed on working hard and its relationship to being well (discussed in

the preceding chapters). Whether or not school leads to an easier life, an argument can be made that, for people in Santa Cruz, an easier life does not necessarily mean a healthier life.

There are many young parents who are also measured in their discussions of the balance between school and working the land. Wanting to offer their children all the opportunities possible, they are quick to recognize that school should not be at the expense of learning how to work the land. Victoriano recently moved back to Santa Cruz because he missed having his own corn. His wife ill with diabetes and high blood pressure, he welcomed the opportunity to grow his food again. When I asked him about his plans for his son for high school, he pragmatically responded.

"I want to send him. If he doesn't do it, there is still the bush to chop." Parents of primary school aged children are overwhelmingly positive about wanting to give their children the opportunity to go to high school if the children make the grades and are able to pass their courses. While they encourage their children, many parents like Victoriano, do not perceive farming to be necessarily a second-rate alternative. Even Esteban, the father of the current valedictorian of the primary school graduating class, was pragmatic about high school, making sure to teach his son what he needed to know about keeping a farm in the village. He explained that he was going to encourage his son to go to school because he wanted to do it but he felt that farming knowledge was important and many days I would arrive at his home to find him and his son out in the farm together. Like the other middle-aged fathers he explained the pragmatics of keeping your options open.

"If you don't go to high school, well then you will know what days are good to chop and plant," he told me, sharpening his machete on a bench in front of his home. He recognized the value of both new knowledge and traditional practice. Another father spoke to this joint value in his answer to the same question about what he would like for young people to learn:

> I want to see young people today work on the land and to take care of the land. If they just misuse the land, the land will be damaged. Looking at other villages, they do not care the way they are using the land. Again when it comes to using of chemical, most chemicals kill the trees that serve from 20 to 30 years. Then changes do come. The future generation should not continue the use of chemical. If they do continue to use chemical today, in the next 20 to 50 years from today there will be changes with the land. We won't see trees but grass. So the younger generation should cultivate the land in a manner that it does not hurt the environment. What I mean by environment is the trees, stream and other things found around us. — Basilio Teul

While he does not mention school specifically, his answer points to the importance of traditional land use and how it becomes viewed as ecological heritage. How to use the land as it has been successfully used for many years is knowledge that is clearly valued in Santa Cruz yet it is not taught as part of the standard school curriculum. There are efforts to forge the divide between school and traditional land practices. Local activists and teachers formed Tumul K'in Center of Learning, a high school located in Blue Creek village dedicated to the integration of traditional Maya land use practices, along with other heritage practices, into the curriculum. Additionally, primary school teachers from throughout the district have formed a group, the Congress of Maya Teachers (CMT). One of the objectives of CMT is to integrate relevant ecological and cultural heritage knowledge into the school curriculum. Pablo Mis, a local Maya activist and educator, was instrumental in the early formation of CMT. When teachers at a meeting to discuss the "spelling Maya," a spelling bee using either Mopan or Q'eqchi' words, suggested that the prizes for winners could be more mainstream or modern than the pig and chickens suggested as prizes, Mis made the importance of the land/school connection explicit.

"For 500 years, we've been told we're a backward people," he explained, going on to clarify that there is a gap in education that Tumul K'in fills and the giving of the animals as prizes also helps to fill that gap, to give value to traditional practices. The giving of animals also, he explained, reinforces the collectivity involved in Maya learning and Maya community life in general. Formal education systems emphasize the individual and individual achievement, whereas Maya values support collectivity and learning through helping and collaborating. A mother's response to the same question discussed above expresses the value of emphasizing collectivity:

> I would want to see the young people today learn how to work together, work at the farm, know how to plant fruits/ground food, learn how to plant and harvest and how to make their own house. It is important for the young people today to learn these because they don't have the knowledge like the ancient people have before. They don't really know what to do so there is the importance for them to learn these and consult with the elders. They need to seek advice from theirs about how they should work together on their land. — Vernancia Pop

Vernacia's desires support Mis's explanation above and seem to sum up the fundamental disjunction between formal schooling and traditional practice in Belizean Maya communities. His efforts, and those of his many colleagues and collaborators in Toledo, seek to address this disjunction. The following section highlights my contribution to those efforts and, in doing so, illuminates some of the ways that children negotiate how and what they learn in and out of the classroom.

TEACHING TRADITION: CURRICULUM BACKGROUND
AND PILOT PROGRAM

Education was my first pathway into social life in general and, more specifically, ecological and cultural heritage and wellness intersections. I first came to Santa Cruz as part of a collaborative project, my contribution being to design and teach lessons to the students in both Santa Cruz and San Miguel, which were initially based primarily on ethnoecological data collected by Rebecca Zarger between 2000 and 2002 in three Q'eqchi' Maya communities in Toledo and follow up discussions between 2004 and 2007 with educators, activists, and non-government organizations throughout the district and with the Belize Ministry of Education. These discussions led to the development of the education plan for the NSF funded collaborative project (Zarger, PI). The lessons included many aspects of Maya cultural heritage, with initial iterations emphasizing traditional plant knowledge drawn from a database of more than 200 ethnobotanical specimens collected by Zarger. I was taken on as part of the team, in part, for my previous experience integrating environmental and science curriculum into a more formal education environment, giving me an advantageous window into the intersection of formalized education and environmental and cultural heritage knowledge and, to some extent, practice. Initially, classes were offered to all children in Santa Cruz, in Standard II and above, on Saturday mornings in a school classroom. Attendance was voluntary. In San Miguel, classes were offered during the school day with middle division elementary students, as was convenient for teachers.

When I arrived for the first day of class in Santa Cruz, the children were waiting. They ran to greet me, eager to carry the papers and pencils I had brought for the lesson. This enthusiasm continued through that day's activities and, in large part, throughout the three years in which the sessions were held. The children, as with any activity, had mixed motivations for coming to class. Most seemed to welcome the change in their daily routine and being given permission to come to class often meant that they were excused from some of their morning work at home. Others seemed to see the classes as an extension of their school experience and, clearly enjoying school, were excited to come to school on Saturdays. Most children seemed to enjoy the subject matter and were as excited to teach me "about the plants" as I was to facilitate their activities. They relished in seeing photos of plants that they had heard of or that they recognized in the booklets we had prepared for them. They brought me leaves and fruits to try and urged me to increase our scheduled number of field trips so they could show me where important plants grew, how they looked or how many there were. I was an attentive student and, as their teacher, carefully supplemented their interests with activities and information that brought what they taught me into a more formal school

setting. This proved a successful formula, with students consistently filling the classroom and parents pleased that their children were being
taught about useful plants, their Maya heritage and the landscape.

The irony of my teaching these topics to students while I was in Santa
Cruz learning about them myself was not lost to my reflexive anthropological gaze. In the context of the consideration of the construction of
heritage, I, through these lessons, was adding value to these topics of
traditional land use by taking them from the bush and into the classroom.
While the critique of this addition of value is not to be ignored, it is
nevertheless a reality that school-based knowledge is somehow experienced as more valuable, regardless of its utility or relevance. This is likely
a post-colonial effect exemplified in the reference reported in the previous section about the history of Maya people being considered "backward." Giving value to indigenous knowledge is not a new pursuit
among scholars critiquing educational systems worldwide. In Belize, the
desire to use traditional knowledge, which was not just useful in the past
but is still currently useful, as a way to supplement the existing curriculum, has often been raised by activists and educators. The process of
circulating this knowledge from the community members and elders,
who share it with me and us, in turn, develop it into activities and share it
with their children adds to these efforts, while also disseminating research findings back to community members. For more details on this
process, please see Baines and Zarger (2012).

LEARNING AWAY FROM THE CLASSROOM: HERITAGE VALUES

As I sat in my hammock listening to a friend talk about how he was going
to try to plant rice in the coming season, hoping to sell it because he
needed to pay for school clothes and books for his daughter starting high
school, I was startled at the realization of another manifestation of heritage change in the face of formal education. I reflected back on my
friend's rice-planting plans in light of a conversation I had later that same
month with Victor Cal, a local educator and Maya activist. We were
discussing a project several high school students at Tumul K'in Center of
Learning had undertaken working with local healers and identifying medicinal plants in the surrounding forest. The students, moved and educated by the project, were now reluctant to clear more forest than was
absolutely necessary for fear of destroying the abundant biodiversity in
the area. Now that they knew how useful so many plants were, they did
not want to chop them. The increased need for money among the subsistence farming families in the villages meant that more and more forest
was being cleared to grow cash crops, for example, rice. Traditional ecological knowledge, in this evaluation, was essentially bearing the double

burden of formal education and the botanical diversity loss derived from attempts to fund that education.

While Santa Cruz was generally considered to be rich in terms of its land quality and botanical diversity, increased high school attendance stirs fears that it could be led to a situation like that described above. Money for school was easily the most discussed reason for parents to look for ways to increase their income. While tuition is generally subsidized by the government, books and uniforms are not. While some scholarships are available, they never cover the cost of school lunches. Food is a powerful indicator of heritage. Children from the villages are reluctant to carry tortillas from home for their lunch, preferring to buy rice and beans, or a similar meal, from the vendors near their school. Speaking with parents and students about this preference and its resultant need for daily money, it was clear that a convergence of factors was responsible. Corn tortillas are an immediate indicator of "Mayaness" and children seem embarrassed to be singled out as different in this way. The tortillas that are so crucial to heritage and health in their villages are rejected as part of school day. While most students, some sheepishly, admitted to this, others claimed that they left too early in the morning to grind corn and make tortillas and that the work was too hard for their mothers to make both breakfast and lunch for all the children before the school bus passed at 5:30 am. While there is certainly truth to this latter explanation as well, the former was the reality for many. It is easy to understand the local frustration in chopping additional forest to plant rice to sell the rice to pay for your children to buy the rice at school. If the irony were not so critical, it would seem comical (Figure 5.1).

This irony demonstrates the difficulties in negotiating, constructing, and embodying ecological heritage. "Within this web of experience, all beings are enmeshed through everyday encounters that are fundamentally embodied" (Miller 2011: 81). While Miller, in her discussion of the materiality of corn in the Amazon emphasizes "being" rather than "learning" as fundamental to the meshwork, the ecological interactions she discusses are certainly process-oriented. The heritage concept used in this study works well with Miller's discussion of materiality in terms of its tangible nature. Traditions are not simply ideas but also "things." When ecological heritage is embodied, it is essentially owned by the individual in a physical sense. It is learned with the body through the acquisition of skills and the experience of the journey to acquire those skills.

"You have to know it and learn it." Hilario was talking with me that afternoon about making sugar from cane. Over the course of many months, this practice had come to light as both a symbol of Maya heritage and a current concern for local residents. People had explained to me about traditional sugar-making practices and a few farmers still grew the cane in their fields. When money was tight, people lamented how they never watched their grandparents to learn how to make sugar or how the

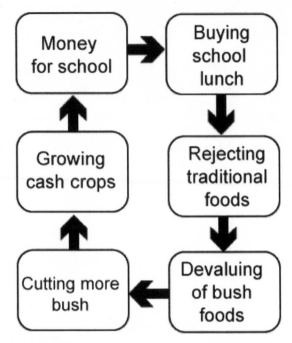

Figure 5.1 Phenomenological Processing Loop: School Lunches

younger generation was too lazy to put in the hard work that sugar making entailed. It was not until sugar became scarce and shops in town began to refuse to sell it to villagers, that the discussion became ubiquitous. Rumor had it that Guatemalans were paying top dollar for the sugar so it was being sent directly to the border, leaving none for villagers, who relied on sweetened tea and coffee as a daily staple, to buy. Until the sugar crisis, there was a sense of pride in families if they had carried down the knowledge of sugar-making practice, even more if they had actually seen it done recently or tasted the "natural sugar." The element of pride and the almost wistful way in which many people spoke about making sugar gave it heritage status. Not only was sugar "a very important tradition" but it also represented an independence from the market economy and a time when Maya people did not need to go to the shop, using the land for all of their needs. With the unexpected sugar crisis, making sugar from cane suddenly moved from being heritage knowledge to a really practical thing to be able to do. Plenty of people knew it, but they could not do it. As Hilario said, "you have to know it *and* learn it" (emphasis mine).

Learning, in this context, involves not simply knowing, but also doing. Knowledge is embodied through practice. While scholars have understood that this is one of the reasons that attempts to collect and record TEK are, in many cases, fundamentally flawed, methodology for describing and analyzing instances of "learning-in-context" is still in development (Zarger 2011). Cajete (in McGregor 2005) clarifies, "building on prior learning and traditions is never a direct or linear path." Particularly in indigenous communities, they are negotiated "through fields of relationships and establishment of a sense of meaning, a sense of territory, a sense of breadth of the context." In the previous chapter, I outlined how work practices are "enskilled" and become embodied knowledge. In the case of sugar making, the practice has slipped away because the knowledge had never been translated into the skill. While the traditional knowledge was present, the embodied heritage was not. While the making of sugar from cane became an increasingly prominent example of the importance of learning in situ, the differences between knowing and doing we evident in a variety of ways.

"Want to grow more foods around the house, whenever you start to do, somebody has to teach you," a younger woman was explaining to me why some of the traditional practices of her grandmother's generation, for example, growing lemongrass and calabash near the home, were not as frequent as in previous years. Her comments speak to the way both teaching and learning happen. First you start to do, and then somebody teaches you. In learning, through practice situations, I observed that children begin a task that they are ready to learn, they "want to try it" and, after this, parents will offer some instruction, either explicitly or by example. Girls as young as two years often sat next to me to bake tortillas or wash clothes, their hand moving in familiar patterns, easily more adept than mine, as I stumbled through my tasks, embodying years of formal schooling devoid of these skills. Never did I observe a mother attempting to explicitly teach a toddler how to bake or wash, they simply tried these tasks whenever they were ready. Afterward, if the mother felt they were ready to learn, they would teach the more nuanced specifics of the tasks. In this sense, learning happens by doing first and learning later. My observations in this regard were also supported by Maya educator and activist Filiberto Penados, who explained to me he and his colleagues' struggles with how to teach Maya knowledge in a formal school setting when Maya knowledge is traditionally not taught at all, but learned when the child is ready to do what it is that is necessary to learn. This additional disjunction between formal education and Maya life, however, does not deter parents from supporting education and students from excelling.

My interviews with the adults in Santa Cruz, in addition to the daily struggles I observed while living there, confirmed that there is no easy answer when it comes to negotiating the formal education system. Education cannot simply be exalted or demonized. Balance is difficult to achieve, with education necessitating many hours to be devoted to its practice, leaving little time for village "work." Bringing formal education and everyday work together into some kind of coherent learning experience seems like a way forward: one which Maya teachers and activists, together with our project, have been pushing toward. The degree to which formal education has a potent effect on traditional aspects of Maya life continues to be debated with conclusions that there is "variation in complexities from one context to another" (Baines and Zarger 2012: 69). Education is but one of the conduits of ongoing or social change in Santa Cruz. The next chapter explores the increased complexities of a changing environment through a discussion of how development is experienced from a phenomenological perspective in Santa Cruz and how this is related to heritage and health among its residents.

SIX

Changing Spaces, Changing Faces: "I Could Not Live Where There Is No Jippy Jappa"

I wasn't sure if there was really fog rolling into the kitchen from the river that morning or if the haze was just the result of my sticky contact lenses after my two hours of sleep on the floor of the bride's bedroom. The open kitchen was still a flurry of activity as it had been for most of the night. Jose leaned against one of the posts supporting the structure's thatched roof and groaned, his hand on his stomach.

"I feel a little bit bad," he offered.

"Why?" I asked.

"My stomach is paining me. Maybe it was from eating the pig last night."

We had driven the two and a half hours from Santa Cruz to Maya Center for his sister's wedding and had spent the previous afternoon and evening preparing meals for the family and the guests. Two pigs had been killed the day before and everyone had eaten well: chicharron and the tripe, accompanied by mountains of tortillas and rice. This morning, work was still in progress: turkey, chicken, the pig meats were all being processed in preparation for the arrival of the wedding guests after the service. The ladies had been working virtually non-stop to not only prepare food for the guests but also to keep up the energy of all the visiting family and friends who were helping with the many preparations. I felt tired but well fed and joyful at being caught up in the flurry of work and family and the latest in Belizean late-night formal hairstyling. It struck me as unusual that Jose would be ill like this at this time and I was interested to know more.

"The pig? You like to eat pig, no?" I inquired. Although Santa Cruz was particularly known in Toledo for the practice of keeping local pigs (and allowing them to roam freely through the village), there were some residents who I knew did not care for pig meat. Jose, however, was not one of them.

"Well, we brought it here and when we tied it, maybe that's not good." He went on to explain that we had placed a lot of stress on the animal when we had transported it the day before. Indeed, the process of tying the pig's legs and hoisting it in the truck had been quite a frenetic experience. The subsequent hours in the back of truck on the highway would have not done much to improve the pig's stress level. He explained that it was not just the stress of the transportation on the pig that made its meat difficult to digest, but also that the act of eating food that was used to a different environment that may have contributed to his illness. The pig was not local and, therefore, its meat was incompatible with the area.

Jose did not let his illness interfere with the work to be done. He decided that he would drink some *caldo kash*, the chicken soup commonly thought of as one of the best "Maya foods" and continued with what he was doing. While much of the work to be done by the men had been completed the night before with the processing of the pigs, men were still involved in building the palm archway for the newlyweds and setting up the stereo system. There was also the heavy lifting to be done in the form of the retrieval of the cases of soft drinks for the guests. The men, too, would have the opportunity to attend the wedding ceremony at the church, whereas most of the women would stay behind and continue preparations for the guests.

At the bride's request and armed with my camera, I attended the ceremony. Peering in to the small wooden church, I was surprised to see the light-skinned officiate speaking English from the platform at the front. I was jostling for a clear camera angle with several other ladies hoping to catch a glimpse of the happy couple. There were seven happy couples this morning, all dressed in full formal wedding attire: brides in long, white lacy dresses and grooms in black suits. The oldest couple appeared to be in their sixties and had raised their family together for decades. I learned that the ceremony was a result of the Nazarene church's efforts to encourage committed but not-officially-married couples to marry. Watching a grandmother sitting in a long white wedding gown and veil brought the disjunction of places and people into sharp focus for the second time that morning. Albeit in very different ways, both Jose's explanation of his stomachache and the new bride grandmother represented a convergence of Maya traditional practice and a less traditional, more modern approach.

Although his sister's wedding was not traditional in that it did not take place in Santa Cruz, her home village, and she was already a mother and living with her husband-to-be, it was clearly important to her that much of the practice associated with traditional Maya weddings be part of hers. Along with the pig, the family brought sacks of corn and other foods from the village. Her sisters and close friends came to kill and prepare local chickens rather than buy frozen white chickens. Her parents came to meet her husband's family in the traditional discussion the night before the wedding. Visitors and helpers were generously fed with a constant supply of meals generated through a collective effort involving countless trips to the river to wash corn, pig guts, and dishes, carried in buckets and basins down muddy banks and meticulously tended to. Although the river and the corn mill were further away and we rode to the church along the highway in the project truck, this wedding celebration was much like any celebration in Santa Cruz.

While the celebration was joyful and the party went off without a hitch, I could not help thinking that Jose's illness, and, importantly, his explanation of it was an indication of how difficult the negotiation of how to retain those traditional practices that are particularly important while outside of a particular landscape or location and while concurrently embracing all that a new location or opportunity has to offer. Traditional practices, as each chapter discusses, become important for a meshwork of reasons: their heritage value, their practicality, economics and, as I argue, their contributions to wellness. In this case, all these factors seem to have come into play. Changing locations is one way in which these practices are modified; however, there are many factors that influence these changes.

This chapter discusses changes in knowledge/practice/perceptions related to health and environmental practices under the umbrella of "development," taking into account the problematic and nebulous nature of this term and highlights, through specific ethnographic examples, how practices are touched by more generalized development processes. This is not intended to be a complete discussion of development or development anthropology but rather uses the umbrella of development to focus on changes, and the negotiation of these changes, affecting behavior and, therefore, I argue, wellness in Santa Cruz. For these purposes, development is defined broadly as "planned social change" (Purcell 1998). It should be noted that, with reference to this definition, there comes an awareness of my disciplinary history with regards to research with indigenous communities and development processes and its roots in "humanistic unease with the effect of westernization on indigenous peoples" (Purcell 1998). This noted, westernization, or globalization if preferred, continues to occur and this chapter highlights some of the possible connections and correlations associated with the changes it brings.

While Belize in general, and both the Toledo District and Santa Cruz village in particular, have been particularly adept in avoiding some of the more heavily critiqued hallmarks of the development process, they are certainly not "untouched." There are no fast food restaurants in Punta Gorda (PG), the closest town, and no tractors and fertilizers in Santa Cruz. Conscious resistance is a partial explanation but, in some respects, Toledo is perceived as the "forgotten district" in terms of government-funded improvements. This chapter takes a phenomenological approach to the implications and negotiations of development, challenging the default linear approach of both its advocates and its detractors. It illustrates ways in which development processes in present-day southern Belize are "spatial, tactile, visual and aural experiences" (Haines 2012).

THE MORE THINGS CHANGE, THE MORE THEY STAY THE SAME

It was on the same highway, traveling north in the project truck and passing very close to the village where the wedding was held, that I had first come to clearly consider the importance of location and land to wellness in the context of development. I was on my way to Belmopan to renew research permits and had been asked by several members of the village if they could have rides to visit family members who had settled in the numerous primarily Maya villages along the road. After much negotiation, the truck was full to safe capacity with representatives from many different Santa Cruz families anticipating rare visits outside of the Toledo District. Transportation costs are prohibitively high to visit as frequently as most people would like.

Over the course of the drive, conversation turned to the pros and cons of living in Santa Cruz versus one of the villages in the area where we were traveling. As might be expected in a generalized development model, villages along the paved highway and closer to the capital city tended to be less traditional. In the Belizean Maya context, this means that their residents tend to work for wages more frequently and practice less subsistence farming. Their location provides them closer proximity to larger towns, resorts, and commercial farms and minimal land suitable for farming. I was told on numerous occasions that, because of this, they eat less corn tortillas and more flour tortillas and rice, products more easily bought at the shop. Passing through, the ladies' clothing seems to reflect this level of tradition, with store-bought items more immediately visible and those made in the villages seeming scarcer. Visits from relatives to their families in Santa Cruz reinforced these observations, with members arriving in jeans and requesting rice instead of corn tortillas while discussing the lack of amenities, cold beer, for example, available in Santa Cruz.

As we drove, it was clear that there was a certain familiar allure of these villages. The children were excited to watch television with their cousins. The ladies were looking forward to cooking on their sisters' gas stoves. Perhaps some of the men were eager to have a cold beer from the bar with their uncles. My friend was sitting in the front seat and an active participant in the conversation. I asked her if she would ever consider moving her family to one of these villages to be closer to her extended family there.

"No." She shook her head and smiled through her nervous laughter.

"Why not?" I probed. Her relatives had been successful there and she clearly missed them.

"They don't have jippy jappa or *tutu* (jute) there. And the creek is hot and it's far."

"Those things are important, then?"

"Yes, Kristina. I could not live where there is no jippy jappa." Her reply was emphatic and carried particular weight because she was not an elder in the community. She had young children and was in her early thirties, young enough to have completed primary school (of note, with high marks). Her life, she stated clearly, was tied to a small palm tree found in the high bush. She was not alone in this sentiment; however I was still surprised by her response. While the shoot from the jippy jappa is delicious, it is hardly a staple food and is unavailable for half of every month. There are other bush plants (almost) as delicious and with similar sorts of availability and I had never heard anybody talk about not being able to live without them. I wondered if the jippy jappa palm was symbolic in some way; perhaps it had become a heritage symbol of sorts, representative of the bounty of the high bush and a connection to that certain environment. This seemed to be reinforced by her initially listing the jippy jappa along with jute, or river snails. I had noted that river snails were mentioned with a high frequency when people spoke about traditional foods, disproportionate to the number of times people seemed to actually eat them. Jute, however, was not mentioned with such high frequency as jippy jappa. Explaining this discrepancy highlights a curious insight into ecological heritage and the changes in how it is created and embodied.

The jippy jappa palm is used almost every day in nearly every household in Santa Cruz. As I mentioned previously, it cannot be harvested every day of the month and is not eaten with notable frequency. It is used to make baskets. These are handmade baskets crafted by Maya women from traditional forest materials; the fronds and shoots of the jippy jappa. These baskets are almost never used in Maya households and are exclusively made to sell to tourists. This practice, I would argue, is not traditional in the sense that I have used the term throughout this study. Maya communities have been weaving baskets for hundreds of years, however, a very small number (three, at my latest observation) of households in Santa Cruz use woven baskets (made from the basket tie tie plant) for shelled corn, beans, and other foods, with the remainder buying plastic baskets for these purposes. The weaving of baskets from jippy jappa was, the story goes, a skill taught to a small group of Belizean Maya women who were invited to Guatemala in the 1980s to learn the practice. Many Guatemala Maya women share a long and rich history of weaving. This particular project was implemented in response to two primary factors. First, in Guatemala, the lengthy civil war left many women without husbands and the need to financially support themselves and their children. While this factor did not apply in Belize, the second factor was salient. Projects had been undertaken throughout both Belize and Guatemala to supply Maya villages with mechanized community corn mills, thus freeing up a considerable amount of time for women that was previously spent in the grinding of corn for each meal. With the increasing desire to take advantage of the market economy, women now had the time to make baskets and sell them for cash to buy goods. Weaving baskets by hand with jippy jappa from the high bush is, ironically perhaps, a response to the technology and desires of development.

Although the practice of making jippy jappa baskets is not traditional in the sense that it has a relatively recent origin, I would argue that it can be considered a heritage practice. Essential to the definition of heritage is the element of construction. For many of the women in Santa Cruz, making jippy jappa baskets is a very important part of their work practice. The processing of the palm fronds and shoots for the baskets is dependent on husbands fetching the raw materials from the bush and connects both women and men to bush materials. Women have told me about asking their husbands who are "lazy to go" to the high bush for the materials and this task being the impetus for them to make the trip. It is a heritage practice, then, in the sense that it involves the collecting of wild plants and reinforces a connection to the landscape even if it is a newer iteration of this connection. For many women, making jippy jappa baskets is one of the only ways in which they can contribute to the household in terms of cash production and the sense of modernity that comes with this responsibility is palpable. Women are proud of the quality of their baskets reflecting pride in a shared Maya heritage. Through the reappropriation of weaving skill as an important Maya practice, women in Santa Cruz demonstrate the flexibility of the heritage definition and counter-intuitive ways in which developmental changes affect heritage practice.

I was mulling over the nuances of these possibilities as I continued our conversation for a while until we reached her family's home and she got out of the truck. As she walked over to the home, I noted that the houses and arrangement in this area of the village looked, at a casual glance, very similar to Santa Cruz. Thatch houses walled with wooden planks sat on small expanses of grass, either one or two in close proximity of one another. I could see a small creek nearby, bisecting the village. Later, when I arrived in Belmopan and dropped off my other passengers, I drove through an area that was visually similar again, with thatch houses and a creek, albeit without the surrounding forest. On the surface at least, the essential elements of a Maya village seemed to be present. What was missing, of course, was both the ability to collect wild plants and animals and the land available for cultivation. Most of the Maya households in Belmopan had a number of residents who had moved to the city from villages and worked for wages in the local shops and hotels. Balancing those aspects of village life, bathing in the river, for example, which are considered essential and, I argue, healthful to being Maya with the different aspects of living in a more urban area without access to land is a complex process.

While my windows into this negotiation offered only brief glimpses, it is significant that almost every family shared with me accounts of time they had spent away from Santa Cruz or relatives that lived away. Oftentimes, particularly after harvests, sacks of corn or other staples would be sent on buses to these relatives, with explanations that the village products were better than any that could be bought. Foodstuffs from the particular village where a family had come from were especially sought after, reinforcing this connection to the land. Although tortillas could be bought in Belmopan and other more urban areas, those made from the corn brought or sent from the village was referred to as "best." In this sense, development processes that manifest themselves in family members moving to less forested and more urban areas may actually serve to reinforce the importance of traditional Maya practices and increase the value of traditional products, corn as a potent example. Not only are these products called for by family members living "out" but there is also a growing market for the sale of these products. Maya people living in "town" form an increasing pool of customers for village-grown foods, in addition to the wild, gathered foods discussed in chapter 3. Again, this illustrates how the "toward development, away from traditional practice" linear conceptions are more nuanced than at first observation. This section was not intended to argue that moving from Santa Cruz does not result in loss of traditional practice. By all accounts, it does. However, I have attempted to illustrate, once again, that heritage is comprised of more than just traditional practice. It is embodied through ecological connections that are flexible and practiced in ways that may not be immediately obvious. In this sense, development need not be an enemy of heritage; however, caution is still advisable in its embrace.

Beyond broader political manifestations and implications, I would argue that the answer to the "cannot not want development" aporia (Wainwright 2008: 12) lies in the discovery of ways in which individuals interact with their environments in ways that reflect both years of development pressure and years of resistance through continuity—a pragmatic and fluid way of interacting on an individual and community level (Wilk 1985). My arguments for this perspective and the data provided here by no means discounts the all-pervasive nature of development pressure and political change, they simply refocus the discussion to the physical realities of daily life, which are deemphasized or missing in political economic accounts. The following example illustrates this further.

CAN'T NOT WANT: THE PAVING OF THE HIGHWAY

When Joel Wainwright wrote in his critique of development in the Toledo District that we "can't not want" development, he captured a very basic dilemma faced by indigenous communities many places in the world. In the Belizean Maya context, development is checked and, as a result of this, it might be argued that it proceeds relatively slowly, except for those times when it is incredibly fast. A salient example of this is the paving of the road through Santa Cruz. The paving of the road from the Dump junction of the Southern Highway to the Guatemala border, to eventually join the Pan-American Highway has been discussed in the Toledo District, with longtime residents remembering that it was slated to begin almost 20 years ago. When the bulldozers and rollers finally arrived in 2011, by all accounts, they moved quickly sparking much discussion about what the benefits and consequences would be when the paving was finished.

"Well, I think maybe it's a little bit good and a little bit bad." This was a common sentiment in Santa Cruz and it was rare that someone took a vehement "pro" or "con" stance on the road paving issue. Perhaps this was because there was very little anyone in Santa Cruz could do to either promote or stop the "highway coming." In this sense, people could "not want" the road paving but there would not be much point. In terms of an active stance, a community member "can't not want" the highway to come. The same is true in the sense that more closely relates to how Wainwright uses his "can't not want" description. How can the residents of Santa Cruz not want easier access to resources that they desire? The highway will make it easier for students to reach high school and reach back again in the evening in time to help with the evening's work or do homework before darkness falls. With the highway will likely come electricity, again helping students complete homework that is now difficult by candlelight. Easier access to the Guatemala border means easier trade of goods which means more profits and more selection. Although, as the previous chapter shows, there is an acute awareness of the pitfalls of education, it is difficult to imagine how someone would want their high school student to struggle daily. We can't not want to make that easier.

Easier access to Guatemala means easier trade and the potential for more money. It also means easier access to Toledo for Guatemalans with something to sell. Or something to do. Frequently expressed concerns in Santa Cruz about this aspect of the increased access included the perceived desire of Guatemalans to buy or farm Santa Cruz lands and the ease of committing crimes and fleeing. Other unsavory practices and problems associated with easier access to both the border and to the neighboring villages included: the use of alcohol and desire for bars on the road and the dangers for school children and livestock walking along the roadside. These latter concerns were mentioned in every conversation I had about the paving of the highway. Children use the road as a main thoroughfare daily, not only to get to school but to participate in daily activities, such as going to the corn mill to grind corn for each meal and to the river to bathe or wash clothes and dishes. The ability of children as young as four or five years to walk safely through the village without adult supervision was never questioned before the anticipation of the road. If the highway were to facilitate the need for children to be supervised to remain safe on the road, the daily rhythm of life would likely change dramatically in Santa Cruz, where children make up over half the population and are relied on to complete many of the necessary daily tasks. If the highway is also deemed unsafe for animals, this daily rhythm would be interrupted even more. The roaming of livestock, while a contentious practice, is a tradition that serves a specific purpose. Free-roaming pigs eat waste, cleaning the village while saving their owners the cost of feeding them the large quantities of food they require. Free-roaming chickens clean stray corn and small food particles from houses and yards while keeping free from their own waste associated with penning. Threats to both animals and children caused by the highway, and its resultant increases in vehicular traffic, are potential threats to traditional practices.

In addition to threatening traditional practices, the potential increase in vehicles poses a real threat to the physical well-being of all of Santa Cruz's residents. Additionally, the potential dangers of the highway have brought the monetary value of animals and land into sharp focus. With pieces of yards already being torn up and re-appropriated for road use, the question of who is responsible for remuneration in the case of loss of land and potential loss of livestock because of the highway construction has been asked many times in both formal and informal capacities. Many residents feel that it has not been answered satisfactorily. Other questions, including more immediate concerns about the labor hired for the road construction and the storage of the road building equipment, still leave some residents worried about the future. Nevertheless, the highway is proceeding quickly, with paving to the border set to be completed in the upcoming year. Awareness of the potential pitfalls, in some cases, does not dampen the anticipation of the positive changes to come through the ease of transportation. While traveling to school and the market are the most cited reasons for welcoming the road, the ease of traveling to the medical clinic was also listed as important. The road, in this respect, contributes to increased wellness and illustrates how the highway, as an example of a development initiative is "a little bit good and a little bit bad." A consideration of wellness through the lens of development should include a discussion of explicit engagement with the biomedical system set alongside traditional medicinal practices.

HEALTH PRACTICE AND WELLNESS:
THE CLINIC AND "THE BUSH"

On the first day of my longest stay in Santa Cruz, a friend came for a visit. He and I, along with his parents, wife, and children, had had numerous extended conversations about the importance of traditional practices in the past and I would readily describe him as the most vocal advocate for Maya land rights in Santa Cruz, even participating in activist-led visits to Belize City. His family was one of the most traditional in one sense, engaged in many practices that few families still observed, but also willing and able to engage with changing practices, with the eldest child just graduating from high school. When he arrived, he delivered some good news: his wife was expecting a baby. He had come to ask if I would be able to take her to the hospital when the time came. The project truck was one of only two working vehicles in the village. I found the request curious and asked him if something was irregular in his wife's pregnancy. He was unsure of exactly the nature of the problem, only that the doctor had said it warranted a hospital birth. At the time, I did not fully appreciate how frequent this request would be. Indeed, requests for hospital transport for all types of concerns came daily. With this frequency, I was afforded both the significant opportunity to help community members with medical issues and witness the choices and interactions they engaged in with respect to the biomedical system.

While decisions regarding what sorts of complaints were significant enough to allow emergency use of the project vehicle to seek immediate medical care would become increasingly difficult, that day I agreed to assist in the transportation for the impending birth if that was what the family wished. The next week, I saw my friend on the road and he invited me to stop by his house later that afternoon. When I arrived, I found his wife on the bed with a small bundle. The baby had been born the day before in the house. Joy and surprise filled the home as the couple calmly relayed how she had felt a little strange visiting a friend that past afternoon. The couple had walked home from the friend's house and their son had been born an hour later. There was no time, or, as it turned out, no need, to travel to the hospital. The birth was attended by my friend's father, experienced in birth assistance. As I admired the healthy, diminutive boy, I wondered why the nurses had told the couple that it was necessary to travel to the hospital. This request was the first in a series of birth transport requests that many people reported as increasing in frequency. In an attempt to find out why women who, like women all over the world, had long traditions of giving birth in their homes were now eager to go to the hospital to have their babies, I spoke at length with the government-trained midwife in the village. In addition to being the official midwife, Fermina Sho is also the community health worker for Santa Cruz. She explained.

"They say that all ladies have to go for their first baby and then for their seventh and the ones after. It's better if they go for all. What if something happens to the baby or the mother? If the baby dies, then they will arrest me!"

"Who said they would do that?" I asked, shocked at her fear.

"They told me at the clinic, at the training. Now I tell all the ladies to go to the clinic. I don't want to go to the jail."

"But is it better for the ladies to go to the hospital?"

"Yes, it's better. If something is wrong, it's good to be at the hospital."

While I did not disagree with her last statement, I wondered how relevant this powerful advice that was fast influencing practice really was in Santa Cruz. I conducted informal interviews with every woman who gave birth while I was living in Santa Cruz, in addition to speaking informally with all women with young children and did not collect any reports about problems during birth, either for the mother or the baby. One woman who reported that she thought it was better to go to the hospital to give birth, and relayed that to me with a certain pride in her more modern choice, had a Cesarean section. She was unclear about the need for this but, assuming there was a serious problem that necessitated the surgery, this was the only one reported. While birthing at home with a qualified attendant is statistically safer for a mother with normal pregnancies,[1] more and more women seemed to be following advice to birth in the hospital. The health worker's reluctance to assist in home births was certainly a factor but women were vocal about being told by nurses at the clinic that they needed to go to give birth in the hospital. Following the advice of biomedical officials without necessarily a clear understanding of the reasons behind the advice occurs frequently and childbirth practices sharply illustrate this. While it is not without note that this can clearly be seen as an expression of the post-colonial development process in the sense that indigenous people are expected to simply do as they are told for their own good because they have been seen as "backward," it is not universal. I observed resistance to the exertions of biomedical power: young mothers who chose to birth at home with their mothers-in-law against nurse requests, refusing to take pills they were given at the clinic.

There is not a clear delineation between those community members who are subsumed by the biomedical power systems[2] and those who resist them. As with other manifestations of developing systems, engagement with biomedicine is subtle and changeable, with the choices of where to seek health care based on a variety of factors. Access is one of the most potent factors. As was illustrated in the birthing example above, seeking medical care at the clinic presupposes the ability to reach the clinic. This has become much easier in the last three years since the opening of the health clinic in San Antonio, just four miles away. This clinic is walkable, although its distance is still prohibitive in cases of extreme illness or debilitation. The proximity of the clinic makes treatment for colds, fevers, and other illnesses that would traditionally be dealt with in the village easier to treat medically. My access to the project vehicle seemed to facilitate requests for clinic treatment for illnesses that, without vehicle access, would be treated at home. Interested in how village members made choices about which illnesses warranted a clinic visit, I attempted to draw a clear line about truck usage, agreeing to drive neighbors to the clinic in cases of emergency or childbirth only, unless I was already heading in the direction of the clinic for project business. This policy not only enabled me to have time to conduct research (and do my laundry) rather than become an exclusive taxi service but it also allowed me to learn about how the severity and type of illnesses were considered and dealt with in the village.

My classification of emergencies requiring medical care at the clinic and those of community members, fortunately, frequently overlapped. Broken bones, profuse bleeding, and small children with very high fevers or who were listless and had trouble breathing were all emergencies for which biomedical care was sought. In most emergency cases, "mechanical" treatment was sought for setting and casting bones and stitching up wounds, for example. Fevers and general pain and malaise were harder to categorize and, while I was reluctant to prolong any suffering, I relied on a general consensus from the community about what seemed like an emergency. Babies were given much more leeway than adults and, although I was confident in this decision, I was never convinced that it was totally correct. Part of the reason for this was the responses that I received when I asked families (n = 64) about their use of bush medicine as part of the administration of the Environmental and Cultural Heritage Assessment (Baines, forthcoming). Bush medicine, or the use of wild plants prepared for illness, was almost universally associated primarily with the treatment of babies and small children. While I observed adults using bush medicine for their own illnesses many times during my stay in Santa Cruz, the most commonly known and used plants were associated with children's ailments (Table 6.1).

While many families were willing to talk about using bush medicine, particularly for children, others were less comfortable discussing any details of possible usage.[3] Some claimed that they knew little about the plants themselves, preferring just to go to the clinic or the bush doctor when they were ill. "Only the bush doctor know it," "we just buy it," and "sometimes you can't find the direct medicine" were all responses to questions about reduced medicinal plant knowledge and usage. While medicinal plant knowledge is specialized knowledge in the sense that not

Table 6.1. Uses for Bush Medicine (n = 64)

"if something frighten she," "when the baby is scared"

"when children like to cry"

"when children skin dry"

"for earache for kids"

"with babies, vomiting," "know the ones for children's vomit"

"for fevers and loose stools with kids," "when babies have fever"

"used it when children were small," "when our child gets sick"

"cut his head," "cut foot, used bush medicine to stop blood"

"just the ones for bellyache," "guava leaf for bellyache—for children"

"after baby is born"

everyone would be expected to know and/or discuss it, there seemed to be a sense that it is heritage knowledge and is being lost because it is practiced less and less. Community members reported that they "never learned it" and I wondered if the biomedical system was to blame. I reflexively asked myself if I was contributing to the loss of this traditional botanical knowledge through my willingness to give sick babies rides to the biomedical clinic. While the presence of biomedical establishments, their recent increased proximity and their impending increased accessibility certainly play a role in the choice of treatments sought, they were not pointed to as the culprit by many community members. Instead of framing the loss of ethnobotanical knowledge and practice as a consequence of changes in medical treatment choices, it was often framed as a deeper heritage issue, one of religious change.

"When the church they start to come, everything change up." Hilario Canti was one of a small handful of Santa Cruz residents who did not identify themselves as belonging to a religion. He spoke in detail about how he had been a member of various churches but they had become divisive and prescriptive, forcing him to change certain practices and give up others. It was in frustration that he decided not to affiliate himself with any. While his solution was rare, his feeling of frustration at the way in which the community was divided in practice based on church loyalties was not unusual. It was an active member of the Catholic Church who shared with me the most direct insight into the social changes that came along with changing medical practice, or vice versa. It was early evening when he explained, very clearly, how he saw religion as the death of ethnobotanical knowledge. While I understood that he was speaking more pointedly about the Evangelical churches in the village, he included his own in the indictment. Religious practice looms large in any observation of social practice and social change in Toledo but I had not yet made a direct connection from it to clinic choice versus ethnobotanical practices. Wondering about the connection between these variables as it related to wellness, I was once again reminded of the construction of heritage. Traditional ethnobotanical knowledge becomes salient as a heritage practice in response to threats from religion and, to some extent, biomedicine. It promotes wellness not simply as a superior way of treating specific ailments, which it may or may not be, but because it reinforces a connection to the forest, and to a common social norm of seeking treatment from within the community and, through learning over time, understanding that treatment (Figure 6.1).

This example speaks to a broader discussion of the way communities, particularly indigenous communities, can interact with development changes on their own terms, protecting their traditional knowledge through the fluidity of their heritage constructions. If indigenous communities are affected in so many ways by economic structures and forces, as the preceding discussion indicates, it may be desirable or advantageous for them to consider economic perspectives. This need not necessitate indigenous "loss." Studies assessing the degree of "indigenousness" in relation to economic engagement highlight this in subtle ways. Reyes-García et al. (2010) highlight how, although there is a reduction in the level of traditional environmental knowledge (TEK) held by those with more formal schooling (one definitive consequence of development), this reduction was minimized by the use of TEK to make the school curricu-

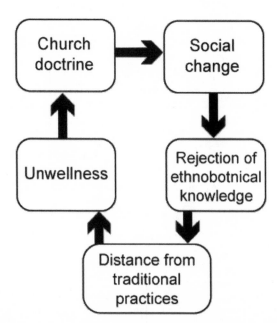

Figure 6.1 Phenomenological Processing Loop: Ethnomedicine and the Church

lum more "contextualized." Anthropological convention suggests that modernization generally weakens traditional knowledge (Quinlan and Quinlan 2007). Zent (2001) notes the reduction of TEK with an increase in schooling associated with development. However, some current evidence suggests that the relationship is more complex (Guest 2002; Zarger and Stepp 2004) and the weakening is less evident as indigenous communities are increasingly engaged in the way their knowledge is conceptualized and used in the development framework (Quinlan and Quinlan 2007). Ownership of both the knowledge and the development process is crucial to a different outcome for the communities involved. This is evident in Santa Cruz through the subtleties expressed throughout this and the previous chapter.

The residents of Santa Cruz engage with the changes the development process brings with both pragmatism and skepticism, and this is reflected in the way they construct their heritage. Johns (1999: 158) begins recognize the nuanced nature of the shifting knowledge base, differentiating between when the changes associated with "modernization" are thrust upon a community versus embraced by them. While he claims that we are not equipped to predict what the consequences of these embraced changes might be, other authors have given this a shot (Lauer and Aswani 2009; Medina 2003). Conceptualizing this ecological knowledge as embodied heritage, as this study does, directly addresses this point, allowing for changes to be incorporated and heritage conceptions to flux in response to those changes.

Returning to the example of childbirth that began this section, I offer a scenario that I observed twice during my time in Santa Cruz. While every mother and every child is different, my observations of these events were markedly similar. In both cases, the young mothers, both close to 20 years, were raised in Santa Cruz leaving to live in neighboring San Antonio with their husbands. Likely, at least in part, a result of living in San Antonio both gave birth in the hospital. One mother was from a Catholic family, the other from a Mennonite family. Together, their stories exemplify the complexities and subtleties of the changes brought by development forces.

"Everything is changing." She was talking about an important postpartum practice of wrapping a smooth rock, hot from the fire, in a piece of cloth to place on the abdomen of the new mother to warm the uterus after child birth. Giving birth in the hospital without their families' support, neither girl had been given a warm rock after their births and both had suffered pain in the days following as a result, they independently explained.

"Young girls don't know about that—that's important—they need that. We still have pain when it's cold." I met with both girls, just a few months apart, at the homes of their respective families. They had returned home to receive the care and treatment of their mothers and grandmothers, who warmed the rocks and brought them to them while they lay in their hammocks. While their upbringings and family lives were very different, at least in part as a result of their different religious beliefs, both dealt with their ailment in a similar way. As the extended families passed the new babies around while the mothers rested in their hammocks, I considered the reach of this traditional medical practice. Embodying this heritage practice seemed to provide much more than simply ensuring the warmth of the uterus. It ensured the wellness of the new mother and her baby in ways that were less quantifiable, perhaps, but no less tangible.

NOTES

1. The World Health Organization (WHO) supported this claim in 1985, and continues to uphold it, working with qualified birth attendants to administer trained birth assistance in the home. The original report states, "it has never been scientifically proven that the hospital is a safer place than the home for a woman who has an uncomplicated pregnancy to have her baby."

2. This statement assumes a background knowledge of the wealth of discussion surrounding biomedical systems and the power they exert. This discussion traces its roots most clearly to Foucault (1973) and his discussion of the "passive body" and has been taken up by many critical medical anthropological theorists and activists in current contexts (see Baer et al. 2003).

3. In my study, I was careful to avoid attempts, or what might be perceived as attempts, to gather detailed information about the use and botanical identity of particular medicinal plants. The appropriation of specific medical ethnobotanical knowledge is contentious and careful studies of healing plant knowledge, including pharmacological breakdowns and studies in ritual administration are currently underway in Toledo with the supervision and at the request of local healers, primarily of Q'eqchi' Maya descent. While some community members were willing to share commonly known and used medicinal plants with me, *yamor*, *secate*, and *nasoon*, as examples, I was careful to respect the extensive knowledge of the local healers and was interested in focusing more on the connections between the community members and these plants rather than the identification and classification of the plants themselves.

SEVEN

Alone, Together:
"You Are Not Afraid?"

She asked me to visit her house that afternoon, sending the request with her daughter. Although I wasn't sure of the exact purpose of the visit, I knew what the invitation was in reference to. News travels fast in a small village, regardless of a desire to leave others to their business. I was simultaneously relieved and anxious. It was relieving to have been invited into the situation in the sense that I desired to offer my assistance if it was wanted. Being invited removed the question of if and when help should be offered. I was anxious because her house was one of the very few in the village that was unfamiliar to me. I had been there only a handful of times, not only because it was set back from the road but also, primarily, because I never felt particularly welcome. I was conflicted and uncomfortable. That day, however, I had been invited and I knew that she would be alone at home with her children. Earlier that day, her husband had been taken into police custody.

When I arrived, she was in the hammock with her youngest child on her lap. It was dark inside and it took me a few minutes before I could make out the bruises across her cheek. I didn't ask any questions, instead letting her tell me whatever she wanted about what had happened earlier that day. It was Sunday and her husband had been drinking. A normally passive and agreeable man, he had a reputation for being a violent drunk. He had beaten his wife before and threatened his children. He had even been arrested before. This time, I sensed that day, was different. As she, the pregnant mother of 10, described to me how her husband had held the loaded shotgun to her face and threatened to kill her before striking her face and body, I felt fortunate that I had been trusted enough to be summoned. This was my eleventh month in Santa Cruz and I knew that I would oblige any requests for help. She needed to reach town to visit the police department and give a statement so charges would be filed against her husband. Without her appearance, she feared he would be released, just like all the other times. There were official visits to make and papers to file at opposite ends of town and the last bus home to the village left at noon. Being pregnant with small children and a primarily Mopan speaker, the difficulties in accomplishing this were great. I agreed to drive her to town.

The next morning, she sat quietly in the passenger's seat of the truck for the first time as we made our way down the uneven road. She had rarely been allowed to travel to town, nor had she been allowed frequent visits to her parents, her married daughter, or any friends in the village. As a consequence, I did not know her as well as I did many of the other ladies. She was quiet but seemed to exude a certain steadfast resolution. I respected her silence, understanding that the decision to take action against her husband, her abuser of twenty years and the father of her children, had to be a very difficult one. It was certainly in violation of the norm of practice. Maya women, according to reports from within and outside the villages, do not typically follow through with reports of abuse.

When we arrived at the mint-green cement block police station on the front street in town, it was still early. Despite the hour, there was a flurry of activity at the station, comings and goings, reports and transports. We stood at the front desk for a few minutes, waiting for the Mopan-speaking officer who was dealing with the case to become available.

"Ms. Kristina! Please. I need to talk to her." He could see us waiting. Her husband was locked in a cell, open to the outside and in the line of sight of the front desk where we were standing. Following her lead, I ignored him. After he called out, each consecutive minute seemed longer than the last until the officer arrived and explained the next steps. She needed to go to the hospital and be examined. The doctor would assess the injuries to her, and possibly the baby she was carrying, and fill out the appropriate paperwork that court would consider when they heard his case. As I sat in the examination room watching the Doppler passing back and forth across her swollen abdomen, I considered how unusually difficult this process must be for her. Being beaten while pregnant is, of course, difficult for any woman but, for her, this difficulty is amplified by a long list of factors. Illustrated in the processing loop (Figure 7.1), her isolation from her community as a result of her husband's controlling violence has meant that she is without the community support or understanding for the violation of the norms of Maya marriage in her giving a statement in support of the charges pressed against her husband. In this sense, if she had been allowed to have more prescriptive behavior in the community, participating in more social events and work exchanges—if she had followed a more customary model of normative action, the unusual assertion of autonomy she was in the midst of might have been better supported. As it stood, however, as she rose from the examination table, her resolution was unwavering and if she had thought beyond her immediate needs and goals, they were not expressed. She was not thinking about her new-found assertions of autonomy against a backdrop of prescriptive "Maya" behavior. She was thinking about her next step.

The baby, thankfully, was fine and the doctor returned a report of "harm" inflicted by her husband's assault. Armed with the report, we made our way back to the police station. We sat on the second floor, looking out across the Caribbean Sea as the salty breezes punctuated her statement. She gave it in Mopan and the officer translated and transcribed. She described what had happened, calmly and in detail, pausing only when the special education class from the school across the street came through the room on a tour of the station.

"This is where mommy comes if daddy beat her," another officer explained to the children as the passed through. A third officer looked up from her desk down the hallway and the officer giving the tour continued, "This is the lady who goes and takes the picture if somebody get dead," he said pointing to the officer at the desk. The kids looked around, some gazing at the incredible ocean view, others taking in the termite-bitten exposed rafters and fraying wires of the room, others still mesmerized at the handsome uniformed officers. She sat patiently, waiting for them to pass through. She slid the paper summarizing her statement in English to me before she signed. It accurately represented the events as she, and others who had witnessed them, had told me they took place. Leaving the police station, we were told to assure her presence in court the next day, when her husband would be charged. She would spend more time in town that week than she had in the past 20 years. Next we visited social services, trying to determine what sort of help a mother of eleven would be entitled to if her family's breadwinner was imprisoned.

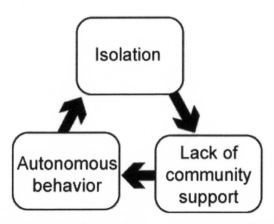

Figure 7.1 Phenomenological Processing Loop: Autonomy and Isolation

By the end of the week, her husband had been sentenced to nine years in the federal prison. While his crime against her was especially heinous, the gun he had used was also unregistered, an offense that often carries a stiff penalty in Belize. A cloud seemed to lift as her bruises healed and I saw her on the road more frequently, visiting her parents and walking with her children. The baby was born without complications. Her eldest sons were able to tend the family farm and bring home some food. Life for her was not without struggle. It is difficult to raise a family alone in a community where you are the only person doing so. Single mothers return to their parents' home, but being the oldest child and having eleven children of her own, this was not a feasible proposition for her, even though she has very supportive parents. However, she never mentioned regret. And sometimes, when we passed each other on the road, I saw her smile.

This vignette both painfully and hopefully illustrates the balance involved in negotiating social life as both an individual and a collective actor, and the relationship of this negotiation to both wellness and traditional practice. This chapter examines the nuanced relationship between the ideas of collectivity and community, on one hand, and autonomy and individual choice, on the other. Throughout the book, I have offered examples of instances when community members have referred to "Maya bodies" or made generalizations about "Maya people." In many ways, through my discussions of heritage and its role in wellness in a broad sense, I have mirrored and supported these generalizations. This chapter critically examines these generalizations, highlighting how individual lived experiences can differ, and how these differences can be supported even when community consensus is high. How choices made by individuals fit into ideas about community action are explored from a phenomenological perspective with a focus on sensory experience. Responses to changing practices and changing definitions of "Mayaness" are highlighted within this discussion.

AUTONOMY AND PRESCRIPTION

I am thankful that the incident related above did not occur in the early days of my time in Santa Cruz. The reaction from community members would likely have been more difficult for me to contextualize and understand. On one hand, there was a clear community consensus that the crime for which the man had been sent to prison was unacceptable and that justice was served. He had violated a prescriptive behavior of the village; he had not respected his wife. However, when people discussed it with me, I heard a kind of deference to the autonomy of the individuals involved that might have stuck me as strange if reference to it was not already peppered throughout my field notes. "Maybe he doesn't want it," mothers would say of children who refused to come inside. "Maybe they don't like it like that," children would say of a family's decisions to make rice instead of corn. "Some they don't do it that way," fathers would say about rotating their fields after planting. When people told me that "he likes to drink and smoke" about the abusive husband, with a shrug of the shoulders, they did not necessarily offer a critique of this behavior. It was offered with a kind of "he likes what he likes, they do what they do" sort of attitude, which might seem incongruous in as homogeneous a place as Santa Cruz. About his wife, I was told several times that his relatives were vexed with me for helping her. Perhaps I, in this instance, had exerted a kind of collective response to what was an autonomous decision. In my field notes, I allude to this confusion: "I haven't actually met anyone who sympathizes with P. but M. (an older man) did say that it might be okay to lash your wife a couple of times with a belt to 'correct her' but (certainly) not to beat her with a gun in the belly when she's pregnant."

What was or was not a violation of normative behavior was based on a barometer that I was still learning how to read. It was becoming clear to me through my participation, observation, and more formal data collections that there was a strong consensus among community members about what Maya people should do to live well and what heritage activities were important in pursuit of this end. Yet, the non-normative behaviors that were explained in terms of personal desire still surprised me. In a subsistence farming community, it seemed strange that children were allowed to "not like" certain foods, and have these desires catered to. Food tantrums were tolerated, ignored even, and referred to as simply personal desires. In a society of limited long-term and large-scale choices, everyday behavioral freedoms were the norm. I found this apparent disjunction unsettling, amplified by my frequent interaction with children acting on their desires during lessons and visits. I augmented my research questions: how did this personal autonomy fit into what I was learning about the importance of heritage and wellness in the community? Given the same environment, how can the data show these strong and widely held convictions about what "Maya bodies" need amid a permissive, "they do what they want" attitude? The following example provides some thoughts about how to go about answering these questions in the wider context.

In chapter 3, I described how the norms of sensory experience are related to both heritage and the embodiment of wellness, using the example of the smells associated with the rituals of the *k'ux* planting. In the same chapter, I mentioned the harvesting and preparation of achiote, which is traditionally used to add the red color to caldo, as an example of a heritage practice on the increase among certain individuals who have responded to a desire for it among Maya people living in towns and villages with less access to land. Here, I offer a further discussion of the preparation and use of achiote (*k'uxub'*) as it relates to autonomous choice and prescriptive behavior through the lens of sensory experience.

Preparing *k'uxub'* is a messy business. The seeds inside the dried pods are covered in a cool red paste that coats and colors fingers with a botanical substance the consistency of thin wet clay. The pods themselves are covered in soft spikes, which gently abrade the damp, red fingers. The color amplifies the soreness from the spikes but the dull pain is only worthwhile if you push through, with each pod yielding only a few small seeds. Tall piles of branches, pod clusters on the ends, fill the corners of the house. Hours pass before there are enough seeds to boil and prepare. There are only a handful of women in Santa Cruz with the time and inclination to deal with this process, however, achiote is used in every household in the village, without exception.

My hands raw from my "in situ learning" about the process, I wondered how anyone would go through this for an ingredient that did not add any flavor as far as I could tell, an ingredient that, nonetheless, was crucial to the preparation of the most important dish for "Maya people." Through my phenomenological lens, my anthropological training still turned my thoughts first to an etic explanation. Achiote, I supposed, must have some vitamin or essential mineral it provides.[1] I wondered if Florentina Pop, my *k'uxub'*-making teacher, had ever considered this as she scrubbed her raw fingers.

"The old people knew what they were doing so it must be good. We learn it like this so the people like it like this. I don't know. It has good things inside? I think maybe yes," she replied to my inquiry.

While not conclusive about the reasons for the use of achiote, Florentina's response is telling, reflecting several elements helpful to this discussion. Her first line shows both trust in elders and an interest in keeping the traditions of the past because they are beneficial. This perspective is not altogether usual, with other traditional practices being dismissed as lacking in scientific foundation. This is discussed in more detail in the next section. Her next line, "we learn it like this, so the people like it like this," gives some insight not only into how preferences are developed but also into the importance of tradition in that development. This also speaks to both community consensus and household variation in asserting that if something is not learned, it will not be considered important. If household members, in response to certain specific environmental conditions, learn practices in a specific way, it follows that those practices will be preferred. There are, of course, additional factors in this process. As other options and other information become available from outside sources, churches, and schools, for example, it would follow that there would be additional points of diversion from the practices derived from the environment. While traditional practices become preferred heritage practices, in this and many cases, through being the best response to environmental factors, other choices exist.

"Some people like the white soup. My husband don't want to eat white soup. I need to buy the achiote." She had invited me for *caldo* and was boiling the chicken when our conversation turned to the preparation and the importance of achiote. From my numerous informal conversations and time spent with her and her family, I would not have described her as a staunch traditionalist. She practiced a relatively new religion from "the States" and she often preferred to speak English with me, something almost everyone in the village would do but much fewer would prefer. The way she spoke about the coloring of the *caldo* made it clear that she knew that there was no "real" reason why the soup needed to be red. The nutrients came from the meat and the garlic and the herbs, the redness was simply a preference. I explained that, in the States, many families ate "white soup" or soup with broth that was uncolored. What was particularly interesting to me was her recognition that there were people who like their soup white, just not her husband. While I never met a family in Santa Cruz that had a preference for uncolored *caldo*, the concession that there was certainly room for variation within a practice that was so clearly an important heritage practice, one that was continued despite its considerable hassle and, to an outsider, very little reward. "Some people" might decide to do it differently.

Adding an explicitly phenomenological perspective to bear on this discussion, I argue here, clarifies how a practice can continue to be prescriptive even though there is discussion of people's autonomous behavior regarding it. For a substance that seemed so initially superfluous, achiote worked its way into my life in many ways. Staring at my red fingers when preparing the achiote was an exclamation point on a year of cuticles stained orange for days after eating *caldo* and futile attempts to scrub those same orange/red stains out of my skirts in the river. Achiote stains do not come out. Ever. Considering this ubiquity, I began to understand the lived experience involved in the practice of coloring *caldo* red. In chapter 3, I described smell as crucial to the sensory experience of the ritual activities associated with planting. I propose that sight provides a similar window into why the adding of the red color persists in the ritual preparation of *caldo*. While individual household variation exists, the preparation of *caldo*, including the adding of the achiote, and the discussion among the elder ladies present of how much color is enough, happens in a very similar fashion across the village. The red color, it might be argued, is a vibrant symbol, denoting that discussion with the elders has occurred and the *caldo* has been prepared correctly. As with the smell discussion, I argue that his practice is beyond simply symbolic but, through the sensory experience of seeing the red color, actually acts on the body, promoting wellness. The physiological changes in response to color are well-documented but beyond the scope of this current discussion. However, the embodiment of this ecological heritage practice is made explicit by the bright red color of the achiote. This sensory experience is an embodied experience and maintained, at least in part I argue, because of its links to wellness. Contributions from the sociality of decision-making, respect for elders and other elements of the ritual experience of adding achiote to *caldo* combine in its construction as heritage. Thus, though autonomy to not need the red color, and certainly to not make it, is freely given, it persists. As each woman mixes and pours the red liquid into the *caldo*, she is participating in a behavior that is prescriptive through her embodiment.

INDIVIDUAL CHOICE AND WELLNESS

"Only that lady know why she feel sick, maybe she no eat." While speculation about the cause of illness was common, today this speculation was accompanied by a dismissive statement about individual knowledge. Individual choice and responsibility, especially when dealing explicitly with wellness, is balanced very carefully with prescriptive concerns about environmental behavior. In the previous chapters, it has become clear that an individual's choice of what they eat is thought to directly relate to their health. "Taking care" of oneself by not getting wet when hot or bathing in the river when it is too hot or dry is also a critique of individual behavior that is thought to lead to ill health. Individuals could choose to behave in ways which were unhealthy but ignoring the traditional ecological practices associated with bathing, farming, and eating could lead to sickness. In order to contextualize the recognition these individual wellness choices have against the backdrop of community health, I offer here a brief assessment of how ideas of the individual, the social, and the ecological have been brought together to bear on wellness from an anthropological perspective.

In his early strides toward assessing well-being in anthropology, Colby (1987) makes an explicit early biocultural attempt to avert the focus away from economic indicators and a nationwide scope, instead looking at the "immediate cultural surround and life-space of individuals." This life-space is defined by cognition related to three worlds: the ecological, the social, and the interpretive. From an evolutionary perspective, in his view, biocultural success should follow if well-being is achieved in these three domains (Colby 1987). Biocultural success, in his program, is measured by longevity. However, longevity, it has been argued since, "may or may not have anything to do with physiological wellness" (Izquierdo 2005: 767).

While Colby relies heavily on measurements of adaptation in his discussion, he implicitly attempts to reconcile what would emerge just a few years later as a central debate in biocultural medical anthropology: the tension between it and critical medical anthropology (Singer 1993; Wiley 1992). Critical medical anthropologists argue(d) that biocultural studies, with their focus on adaptation at the individual, physical level have ignored larger political and economic forces that create structural inequalities, which in turn "create situations in which conditions enhance health and well-being for some social sectors, but, at the same time, cause more sickness for others" (Levin and Browner 2005: 746). Following a call for "critical bioculturalism" (Baer et al. 2003: 15) and the elucidation of the "biocultural synthesis" (Leatherman et al. 1993), which attempted to explicitly add political economic discussions to biocultural research, it can be argued that critical medical anthropology can be considered as part of the biocultural domain, especially in discussion of wellness. Studies linking socio-political relationships to environmental changes to physical adaptations have continued to cross this divide and fuse theories and methodologies (Lende 2005; Dressler and Bindon 2000; McDade 2002; Reyes-García et al. 2010), so much so that considering social conditions when measuring wellness, even when it is confined to changes in physical health, is common among anthropologists of many traditions. Rather than pitting explanations favoring environmental adaptation identified as "biocultural" versus those favoring external social and political forces identified as "critical" versus those favoring the individual, lived experience identified as "phenomenological" there is a decades-long precedent for incorporating each view into building an explanation that reflects the complexities of well-being itself.

This introduces a crucial point of focus in the conceptualization of wellness in this research. Adelson (2009: 113) makes a point that social networks play a vital role in the acquisition of bush foods among her Cree informants. The achievement of well-being, then, is inherently social rather than focused on the individual body and individual achievement. Her point is well-taken and salient in light of the heavy emphasis on individual fulfillment in well-being studies from disciplines such as public health and psychology, however, a point she does not fully investigate is of great interest. The acquisition and preparation of these bush foods correlates directly to individual physical health in terms of access to adequate nutrients. In this sense, measuring nutrient levels may be a direct measure of the social relationships crucial to well-being. Although a few recent studies investigate the importance of land/body relationships, they focus on the social and conceptual nature of well-being, often while highlighting political economic issues, without an attempt at a biocultural "next step" (Mark and Lyons 2010; Adelson 2009). Responses to questions about what makes a person "healthy" or "well," discussed in more depth in chapter 3, often included bush foods and analysis revealed that there was both a bio-physical (related to wild foods being better for the body) and a more complex individual and socio-political (related to "Indian bodies" and heritage) component to these answers. This example illustrates the need for multiple perspectives in understanding Mopan Maya well-being.

While physical health of the biological body is a consideration, ecological adaptation related to wellness has been viewed through a specifically political lens in need of mentioning here. Political ecological studies explore relationships between individuals, society, nature, and, in many cases, health in the context of external power (Escobar 1996; Baer 1996). Power in relation to nature and human well-being is manifested in many ways, ranging from the overt, for example, natural resource extraction and subsequent contamination of indigenous lands by international corporations (Izquierdo 2005; Kirsch 2007), to the more subtle, for example constructing heritage claims and conceptions in Belize. This line of inquiry, exploring the relationship of power to health by way of the natural environment, owes a theoretical debt to the politics of power discussed by Foucault (1976 [2003]). While the Foucauldian conception of the "passive body" being "acted upon" by politicized outside forces is not incompatible with processes of ecological adaptation acting upon the body, its consideration adds an additional dimension to the research process. Notable attempts to side-step explicit political concerns and make connections between ecology and well-being by way of a consideration of direct interactions with the landscape have come from medical geographers (Kearns and Gesler 1998; Brown et al. 2009), with anthropologists beginning to recognize this gap and utilize wider literature to form ideas about how the natural environment affects health on the level of the individual body (Ingold 2000; Hsu 2007). While the external view of the "passive body", as outlined by Foucault (1976 [2003]), and the individual, sensitized phenomenological body, as outlined by Merleau-Ponty (1962 [2002]) and used as the driving theoretical frame throughout this book may seem at odds, Crossley (1996) asserts that they are "compatible and complimentary at both the theoretical and the political levels." This compatibility allows the holistic discussion of wellness to continue.

This discussion leads us to a place where it "all depends to the people, to each family, to each house." I argue, however, that this does not preclude a discussion of how practices become shared heritage and, as such, shared contributors to explanations of wellness. To illustrate, I return to the example of burning incense, a heritage practice that is decreasing, in part because of its rejection by the Evangelical churches.

"My parents never teach me—they grow me in Christian. In San Jose, they do it. I tell my boys, I'll show them but just words." This statement speaks to both the learning process, described in detail in chapters 4 and 5, but also to the variation surrounding the practice. It is important to understand that this is not just a "pro-traditional, anti-tradition" issue divided by religion. There is room for pragmatic decisions that reflect ecological and situational situations. A discussion with a young Baptist man highlights this.

"They put their cultural beliefs in that. Now, some people do it for fun. They don't put their belief in that. They put their belief in God. For fun, for culture. That's not something that's going to make things grow." In this discussion, he does not offer an indictment of the practice but recognizes its importance as a heritage practice, "for culture." He is clear to make the distinction, however, that there is no "real" efficacy in the use of incense, just "fun" or heritage. I argue in chapter 3 that the heritage practice itself creates the efficacy, at least in terms of the health of the people participating. Healthy, happy, well-connected workers, in turn, can lead to a successful planting and a successful harvest.

"If I have it, I do it—in dry or matahambre. [The old people] do it. They talk to the mountains, they know how to say it. They stop when people come from States." A Catholic father of seven describes his choice, based on the pragmatics of having the incense or not. His brother-in-law is more vehement, noting that it is "important to practice our tradition." While, I asked him to qualify this importance, he spoke in the abstract about traditional ways being important for the Maya, the land being important. While he did not use the word, he was speaking about heritage and its value. Even within his extensive exposition of his conviction to burning incense as a heritage practice, he was careful to allow for other individuals to choose not to do it. He, however, worried that the strength of the community would suffer if too many individuals chose not to participate in heritage practices. These fears related to deviations from traditional practices are discussed in the following section.

FEAR AND CHANGE

"You are not afraid?" This happened a lot. I was visiting late into the evening, likely immersed in conversation about the importance of tradition and the changing face of Santa Cruz. When it came time for me to head home, I was almost always asked if I stayed in my house alone. Understanding the importance of working together and helping each other in Maya communities, I understood why this might be considered as strange. It is rare for a Maya person to be alone, and the Western concept of "alone time" is not salient. Being alone is a state to be avoided. Older women whose children are gone from the house or younger women who are unable to have children are often given a grandchild, niece, or nephew to stay with them and help them. People rely on each other and collectivity is valued.

"Well, I have Tuli," I offered, when people asked me if I was afraid to be alone. Weighing in at maybe 10 pounds, I was not sure what my disobedient dog could do for me in the face of danger.

"Why would I be afraid? What should I be afraid of?" I probed. I never received an answer beyond "to be alone." There was sometimes talk of ladies being afraid of "drunken men" but it would be unusual for a drunken man to show up at house randomly and, fortunately, none ever came to mine. The fear of being alone, and my consistent reminder of an expectation of this fear, illuminated for me a fear of both straying from the community norm of living together and a more generalized fear of deviating from an important heritage practice, helping each other. Fears of what might happen to both wellness and heritage if traditional ways are not practiced are set aside, and the understanding that "some people" will do whatever it is they do, incorporating new practices or simply showing diversity in their expression of more traditional ones. A powerful manifestation of the negotiation of changing views of "should be" for community members and the diversity that was curiously tolerated, my common experience drove me to investigate the nuances of the role of both heritage and wellness in perceptions of collective action. This particular investigation into normative behavior was incorporated into a series of interview questions.

I asked specifically about what was important about things that were done in the past and how the community, and individuals, dealt with changes. There were a variety of responses highlighting different aspects of collective heritage practices and individual variation in relation to these. The first makes reference to the collective imperative to engage in ecological heritage practice:

> We do need to work on the land as the Maya people, that's how we survive.—Susano Canti

This need is echoed in responses by younger men, however, there is the recognition of different practices:

> Yes, it is very important to use the land in the old way. In the past the people have a long space of time when they use the land over again. Today, for example, if you clear a piece of land for use, it should have about seven years spacing before it should be used again. However people today do not practice farming that way. They have a corn field and as soon it is harvested they use it over again. It results in grass starting to grow. Long ago the people do use their knowledge wisely.— Raymundo Sho

In his response, Raymundo alludes to the mistakes that some people now make might be avoided if they were to use their knowledge. They have the knowledge but they choose to practice farming differently. This speaks to the autonomy of decision making, even in a situation in which the community could (and, sometimes, does) dictate practice. Because land is community owned, the village council have a say in what farmers can and cannot do with the land. For example, in Santa Cruz men cannot cut pasture for cows, despite some desiring to do so. Autonomy is limited by heritage practice and traditional ecological knowledge in this sense. Policing, however, is difficult and, oftentimes, individuals change protocols and behave in ways that are counter-normative. These practices, even if they are considered "anti-Maya," are sometimes left unchecked. The following excerpt, from a young father of seven, explains the consequences of straying from traditional farming practices while recognizing that most people in his community still follow them:

> It is important; because the old people before don't use any chemical when farming. Ground food like cassava, cocoyam is producing without the use of chemical. They don't just cut down forest trees. They know which trees are ready to be cut. After a crop is produced, they left the land for a good while to grow back to high bushes. Then it is used again. That's an important cycle of using the land. Over all the soil is still good and healthy today. However continuing the using of chemical will bring more changes. — Basilio Teul

Fear of the negative changes brought about through the use of chemicals is echoed in a response from another young father:

> There is an advantage of the way they uses the land in the past. In the past no chemical/fertilizer are used. They only clear the land by chopping which is organic. Today a lot of people use chemicals/fertilizers. This cause water pollution in the land we living now. Some examples are with fishes, pets and other animals dies because of water pollution. — Jose Mes

Changes in the soil and the environment are evident in yields. The following is an excerpt from a woman who has noticed the end result of farming changes in the amount of corn she has to prepare:

> Sometime you will harvest a lot of corn and sometimes not because the soil is not good again. Before, when you plant at the first time like 6 quarts, you will harvest a lot. It's less work for people. You don't need to plant a lot to harvest a good amount. Today you need to make a big farm to harvest a lot. — Valeria Sho

Changes in farming practices facilitate changes in work practices for both men and women. A young mother, who embraces both traditional practices and the more modern elements of shop keeping and educating her children at the university level, explained the differences:

> So it's different with today life. The women use to go left food for the men at the plantation. The men on the other side do work together. Today women no longer go left food at the plantation. After work is done for the day, the men make their way home to eat . . . I would love the way it use to be before, however it is not practiced any longer. The people tend to get lazy and it's no longer happening. They don't believe in working together now. — Vernancia Pop

I participated in the practice of carrying food to the plantation only once during my time in Santa Cruz, with Florentina Pop, my achiote-making teacher mentioned earlier in this chapter. It was a dying tradition. While working together in my experience and in all of the data collected was alive and well as a valued and practiced tradition, Vernancia's fears of laziness overcoming the people were echoed frequently throughout the village. When a friend came to the village to visit me, her first word of Mopan learned was *säkän*, or lazy. By the end of her three-day visit, she was able to conjugate . . . I'm lazy, you're lazy, they're lazy. While the accusation of laziness was often given in jest, or as a manifestation of self-depreciation by women who were quite obviously the opposite of anyone who could be remotely considered to be lazy, the ubiquity of the word is telling. As the opposite of work, laziness is one individual behavior that is not tolerated. Armed with these additional insights, I sought to uncover more instances in which individual choice, change, and autonomy would be reflected or rejected.

CONSENSUS THROUGH DIFFERENCE:
AGREEMENT AND DIVERGENCE

During my final month in Belize, I designed and administered a short informal consensus survey, which aimed to confirm or deny agreement between households on important issues related to heritage and wellness, which had been raised through the multiple data collection processes. I chose seventeen statements, verbatim, from my field notes, which represented topics that addressed my research questions most directly. I asked respondents to answer "yes" or "no" to indicate if they agreed with the statement or did not agree with the statement. While some research protocols recommend the insertion of negatives in some of the statements, others suggest that statements be written as they were spoken by informants. Because of my familiarity to the respondents, I felt confident that they would feel comfortable disagreeing with statements and the insertion of negatives would seem contrived, so all statements were given as spoken. Surveys were administered orally, in Mopan, and, like the environmental heritage and wellness assessment (see Baines, forthcoming), they were given on the household level[2] with at least the female head of household present. In reality, each response represents a discussion and achievement of household consensus. While I am aware that statistical analyses are possible using these data, I have chosen to use a descriptive approach to them in order to add insight to the ideas presented previously in chapters 3 and 6 and further systematically contextualize the ethnographic data. Percentage frequencies are given for the responses and each statement is discussed in the paragraph following.

Good Men Grow Corn
    Yes: 100% No: 0%

After conducting this ethnographic research, there was little doubt that this statement would elicit agreement from all respondents. Although the data presented in previous chapters show that younger people, too, recognize the link between planting corn, I would speculate that if the survey were administered on an individual level, there may be a small disagreement from high school students, a growing number of whom are not planting corn and may still consider themselves "good men." Corn as essential to goodness or wellness persists, however, with even, for example, the children of one of the only three families in the village with university attendees requesting corn from the village sent to them.

When Our Body Is Healthy, Our Mind Is Healthy/Not Worried
    Yes: 100% No: 0%

I reject Cartesian assumptions about the separation of mind and body, using the terms "wellness" and "well-being," often associated with psychological health or overall health, and "health," which has often been reserved for physical health, interchangeably. I argue that the distinction is not as salient in Santa Cruz as it is in the U.S. The answer to this question supports this argument. "Worrying" was given in the list of illnesses, along with illness associated with physical problems or pathogens. Throughout my study, I recognized that the way people spoke about health was inclusive of mental health and happiness and this statement goes far toward supporting this observation. This blurring of the customary lines between different aspects of the well self seems to be in opposition to some newer church teaching. During a sermon at the Mennonite church, I heard that "the Christian life is one of conflict" and "there is conflict between the body and the spirit." While the "Maya life" is certainly compatible with the "Christian life" for many of Santa Cruz's residents, this observation does underscore that any import from "the States" will bear the hallmarks of a Cartesian foundation.

Bananas Come Beautiful If You Plant Them in the High Bush
    Yes: 91.7 No: 8.3%

Bananas were highlighted as one of the "healthy foods" in the data analyses presented in chapters 3 and 6. They represent a more traditional crop, grown for small-scale sale in the village. Men who plant other cash crops, *pepitoria* for example, often report that they do not have time to plant bananas. Of note, bananas also represent one of the few ways in which young men can "work out" of the village, harvesting bananas on commercial farms near the Southern highway north of Toledo. This statement is a commentary, I argue, both on the misuse of land for commercial farming; bananas are not as beautiful or healthy when they come from commercial farms on commercial land, and also on the value of not being lazy and going to the high bush where the soil is traditionally of high quality and the land is rotated. In many villages, there is no longer any high bush. Speaking about the high bush carries with it a heritage cache, a pride in Santa Cruz lands. This statement explicitly connects heritage with the *kich'pan*, or beautiful and healthy qualities of bananas. The slight disagreement with this statement comes from one household determining that bananas are just as good planted nearby.

Yamor Is Good for Sickness
    Yes: 100% No: 0%

There are very few medicinal plants that most everyone knows. *Yamor* is one of these. Its small leaves are made into tea or rubbed directly on the body for stomachache and for cooling the body. It is the "go to" plant for many household, even those who might go on to go to the clinic or a bush doctor. Even if people do not use the plant, they know the plant and would have answered "yes" to this question. *Yamor* is a good example of how knowledge and practice come together to form heritage. People who use *yamor* speak about it as an important traditional practice. Medicinal plants play an interesting role in the development of heritage. On one hand, they are the quintessential examples of TEK that should be saved; however, care must be taken as the documentation of this knowledge can be misappropriated and misused so easily. While, as I stated in chapter 6, did not attempt to document medicinal plant use, a few plants, namely *yamor*, were brought to my attention as people came to know my interest in heritage and health. I heard the use of *yamor* discussed as a sort of cleansing ritual, forming a kind of tonic that the "old people" used to drink every so often to clean the blood. While I saw no evidence that young people were practicing this kind of preventive medicine, they were able to speak to this practice. In this sense, *yamor* served as a kind of heritage example of how the older folks were healthier. From a heritage perspective, *yamor* is an interesting example in that its use is not particular to Maya communities. It is used throughout the ethnic groups in Belize and in the wider Caribbean and, while I did not study this particularly, appears to play a role in the constructions of plant heritage among those groups.

Sweating and Working Help Me Feel Good
    Yes: 100% No: 0%

Again, total agreement with this statement supports the data presented in chapters 3 and 4, which demonstrate the link between work and health. Of note, in light of the discussion of education in chapter 5, is the reference to sweating. Clearly, work is defined in this statement as farmwork rather than office work, which would no normally produce sweat. The value of working the land and the hard labor it requires is repeated here again. Feeling good and healthy after a hard day's work in the farm or by the river and firehearth exemplifies the connections I make explicit in this study. Working the land and feeling good is embodying ecological heritage.

Chemicals in White Chicken Make Me Sick
    Yes: 100% No: 0%

The full agreement here supports my observations and informal conversations, however, even though there is consensus, there is a concession to difference. One of the respondents agreed but then went on to speak about others who ate the white chicken frequently, "it's up to them, I don't think they know that it will kill them." This serves as another example of how a recognition and acceptance of individual choice exists within a consensus.

Tortillas Make Our Bodies Feel Strong
    Yes: 100% No: 0%

Strength and health is linked to the production and consumption of corn tortillas. I attended many meals in which corn tortillas were not present and rarely finished the meal before someone, usually the male head of household, pointed out that, although he liked rice or flour tortillas just fine, he just was not full or satisfied without corn tortillas. The ability to work and have stamina, strength, and health is connected to the eating of corn tortillas.

It Is Important to Live Near a Cool Creek
    Yes: 83.3% No: 16.7%

The middle of the survey showed some disagreement. While this answer supports the importance of the river to Maya life, a small number of households were less convinced that the river was necessary for life. The proximity to the cool river was set against discussion of family that lived in town or other villages where the rivers were not as nice; they were hot and shallow. Because most houses in Santa Cruz paid every month for access to the village water system, or the "pipe," the river access is less essential for the provision of water. Most households with piped water, however, continued to use the river for many of their daily activities.

I Could Not Live Somewhere Where There Is No Jippy Jappa
    Yes: 91.7 No: 8.3%

This statement was discussed at length in the context in which it was first spoken in the previous chapter. That discussion aside, I was still surprised that the consensus was so high. Jippy jappa is an important heritage plant and, according to the majority of residents, living somewhere where it grows and can be harvested is important.

It's Good to Eat Hot Things, Like Pepper, When You Are Pregnant
   Yes: 41.7% No: 58.3%

This was the most contentious question, with over half of respondents disagreeing, many of them actively lobbying for the reverse practice. This inconsistency when it comes to temperature of foods is consistent with my inability to find clear patterns in the way temperature norms were applied. There was a sense that temperature was important as it was mentioned frequently. The responses to this question were passionate. It seems that there are flexible rules for the application of temperature prescriptions. Part of the division in regards to this question in particular likely lies in the mixed messages reaching Santa Cruz in regards to pregnancy and birth, discussed in chapter 6. With food preferences and food restrictions incorporating information from the biomedical system, traditional norms can flex and change.

Children Don't Know What the *Ch'alaam*[3] Looks Like
   Yes: 66.7% No: 33.3%

I would like to think that the disagreement with this response is, in part, due to (positive) project interference and the circulation of the value of traditional knowledge (Baines and Zarger 2012). One third of respondents thought that children *did* know what the plant looked like. As explained in chapter 5, our project, with the support of the community leaders, provided environmental and cultural heritage classes for children in Santa Cruz. One of the lessons included pictures of the *ch'alaam*, a plant traditionally used for making a fish poison to catch fish in small creeks. Parents often complained that their children did not know enough about traditionally used plants and their important plant heritage. It was during one of these conversations that the statement was originally recorded. Heritage practices and knowledge have different value to different families and this question most clearly illustrates those differences that do exist.

Eating Fresh/Local Meat Makes You Happy
   Yes: 100% No: 0%

Supported by both biomedical health professionals and embodied heritage ideals, the benefits of eating local shows full consensus. Of note here is the statement that the local meat makes you "happy" rather than "healthy." In answering the question, people did not hesitate or make a distinction between health and happiness, supporting the assumption, discussed above, that mental health, or happiness, is not clearly distinguished from physical health. When people were interested in discussing the availability of meat and other foods in the States, I explained about the movement toward local meats as healthier choices and, always, was met with agreement.

People Can Take Care of Themselves with Bush Medicine
    Yes: 100% No: 0%

While not all families use bush medicine, there is agreement that it is effective. Interestingly, bush medicine received from a reputable bush doctor can be more expensive than seeking help at a government clinic where basic treatment is free after the production of a social security card. Again, there is some heritage pride associated with the use of bush medicine that extended beyond its practice.

Working Together is the Most Important Maya Tradition to Keep
    Yes: 100% No: 0%

The agreement here is unsurprising. Chapter 4 discusses at length how working together is a crucial social practice and closely related to wellness via several pathways. Through collective ritual experience, through the ability to grow food to feed ones family despite illness and weakness and to keep the body strong through physical labor all contribute to the importance of this traditional practice and its strong heritage value.

Children Are Lazier to Farm Now Than in the Past
    Yes: 91.7 No: 8.3%

Related to the previous question about the importance of traditional work practices, this question reinforces the consensus surrounding problems with "laziness" described earlier in this chapter. While concerns with school seem to link here, there are cases in which parents complain about young people, regardless of their participation in school. Perhaps this is partially a reflection of the cliché that parents always think kids were more industrious in the past. Tied up in this is the undoubted decrease in effort required to meet ones basic needs, the proximity of water with the laying of the pipe and the increase in bus and transportation services, as examples. Whatever the rationale, this statement speaks to perceptions of heritage loss and the value of hard work as integral to the construction of that heritage.

When Children Go to School, They Don't Want Their Traditions Anymore
    Yes: 83.3% No: 16.7%

While this is contentious in the literature, it is often perceived to be the case in practice. The consensus here seems to reflect the community feeling about the issue of education, with the numerical acknowledgement that Santa Cruz has many examples of formally educated children who continue to desire village foods and even return to the village to farm, while the majority have an increased desire to do less traditional work. Heritage construction have a role in this. During my time in Santa Cruz, a recent high-performing high school graduate shared her struggles with me about how she wanted to get a good job but she did not want to leave her village. She seemed to have a certain pride in the beauty and ecology of Santa Cruz, recognition of the positive aspects of living in a more traditional way. She did not want to leave her heritage behind as she moved forward with her work and studies. Finding a way to do this is, no doubt, complex but the desire speaks to their being more than a simple linear relationship that this statement reflects.

Garlic, Pepper, and Oregano Help the Body Get Strong
    Yes: 91.7 No: 8.3%

The one household is disagreement with this statement, countered it with an explanation, which indicated to me the household's extensive involvement with American and European visitors. The male head of household indicated that garlic, pepper, and oregano were just "for the flavor" and it was the soup that these ingredients were added to that provided the benefits for the body. Separating the herbs and spices from the healthful and strengthening properties of the soup seemed strange, particularly given the emphasis on their importance in the preparation of *caldo*. That herbs and spices are healthful is not often communicated in an explicit way, as it might be on a "natural remedies" website in the U.S., however, it is, I would argue, embodied in the heritage practice of the soup's preparation. Like the use of achiote discussed earlier in this chapter, the consensus surrounding the addition of these ingredients to the *caldo* is a reflection of the embodiment of ecological heritage, increasing wellness, as also discussed earlier in this chapter, not only because of the botanical properties of the ingredients, but also the ritual and social practice associated with their sourcing, preparing, and adding to the *caldo*.

    The analysis and discussion in this chapter shows that, although there is a high degree of agreement surrounding broad heritage issues, there is a level of flexibility in individual behaviors that is recognized and accepted. Dressler et al. (2007) in their discussion of cultural consensus modeling "people do not just know or think things, they do and believe things" recognizing that the assessment of the degree to which behaviors accurately reflect their beliefs is difficult. They discuss cultural consonance, which takes cultural consensus model a step further, presupposing that learning takes place within "environments of shared meaning" and it examines how these meanings play out in the lived experiences of individuals. Particularly relevant for my study, Dressler and his colleagues make the explicit connection between levels of cultural consonance and the health of individuals. While my level of analysis for this study does not warrant, or necessitate, a ranking of individual households by cultural consonance level, this relevance remains in the light of this discussion. In my study, I argue for the construction and subsequent embodiment of ecological heritage practices as being related to, and having a positive effect on wellness. Heritage and its constituent parts, traditional ecological knowledge and practice among them, is a cultural domain which, I argue, adherence to has a tangible effect on the body.

NOTES

1. I later found some popular evidence to suggest that achiote may have antioxidant, liver support, insect repellent, and cholesterol-lowering properties.

2. Surveys were conducted with twelve households, chosen using stratified sampling techniques to represent community variation in religion, household size, and level of traditional practice based on the environmental heritage and wellness assessment. The sample was comprised of five Catholic households, five Baptist or related Evangelical households, one Mennonite household, and one household without religion. The average household member size was 5.5, with the smallest household surveyed comprised of two members and the largest comprised of 10. Only the members living in the house at the time were counted.

3. Ch'alaam is a plant used to poison fish in small creeks, for home consumption.

EIGHT

Ending at the Beginning: "The Past Is the Future"

I saw the light coming from behind the high shrubs in front of the houses. It was several hours into darkness, and I knew the people riding in the back of the truck wanted to get home, but I stopped anyway. I told them I would return soon, slipping out of the driver's seat and jumping carefully from grassy patch to grassy patch avoiding the mud. The music was uncomfortably loud through the darkness, amplified through large speakers pointed into the empty space between the two houses, in anticipation, I assumed, of the arrival of many more mourners. A great man, they said, was dead.

I had met him only once. He was uncle of some of my best students in Santa Cruz and a bush doctor with a powerful reputation that extended across many villages. His loss was the subject of many conversations throughout the district. I had just finished having one of those conversations, live on the radio, a few minutes before I stopped the truck on the dark road just before the bridge. It was my final radio show before leaving Toledo; my official fieldwork stretch was just days from being over. The "TEACHA program" was a (mostly) weekly event, which entailed me traveling from Santa Cruz to Blue Creek village to present modified lessons from the project environmental and cultural heritage educational curriculum live on Ak' Kutan radio, a community radio station designed to be the voice of Maya people. Broadcasting to villages who have limited access to other forms of media, Ak' Kutan serves an important role in local Maya communities. The theme of my last show that night was "the past is the future." During the hour-long program, radio manager and host, Aurelio Sho, and I discussed how traditional knowledge was not simply important as history and to celebrate heritage, it was important because it was still a useful and healthy way for individuals and communities to live in their environment.

"And you know about Mr. Choco who passed away?" Aurelio gestured in the direction of the dead man's house at the end of the same road.

"Yes," I slowly nodded.

"Think about all the people he helped with his knowledge of medicinal plants," he continued.

"His knowledge is not lost, though. His nieces and nephews know so much about traditional plants. They have taught me so much. . . ." It was true that the Choco children had been incredibly instructional, finding new plants to show me for years.

The children were the people that I first saw as I entered his house, slightly stunned by the music pumping outside. They had been brought by their parents to be with their aunt and extended family and await his body's return from the hospital and the wake to begin. I greeting them, moving carefully into the next house where his widow was preparing drinks for the visitors. The small room was filled to capacity. About forty people sat on overturned buckets and bancos. They waited calmly, simply providing their presence for the time being, with help with the cooking and serving coming later no doubt. I was struck with the quiet inside the room. Nobody spoke. It is hard to say if the mood was somber or simply matter of fact. When somebody dies, it is customary to come pay respects to the family. Simply spending some time is enough.

The colorful ribbon woven through the braids of the widow gave the outward indication of an adherence to heritage practice. In my experience of many villages in Toledo, only those, primarily Q'eqchi', Maya women with close ties to tradition still wear their hair in that way. As I sat and watched her moving about the room, the green and red and purple flashing across my eyes heavy with the weight of the day, I continued to think about the conversation that I had had that evening back at the radio station. I thought about the gathering I was currently participating in and how it was an example of how traditional practices, which become heritage through a convergence of factors, are described as important for so many reasons. Heritage is meaningfully discussed and constructed in the abstract, as a collaborative force and assertion of one's own history. What we had spoken about on the radio that night, though, is that heritage is meaningful because it serves a meaningful function, perpetuating practices that have been adjusted and refined through interaction with the environment; practices that work. Indeed, the past was the future.

I was not sure how much time had passed when I, again, became consciously aware of my surroundings and the mourners filling the room. As I struggled to focus, my thoughts turned to the people waiting in my truck. Sleep deprivation, I speculated, was an important part of the embodiment of the ritual process of sitting up for the deceased. It, however, was not ideal during the non-traditional activity of operating a vehicle on dark and unpaved roads. I offered the widow my condolences and excused myself, saying good bye to the children through the wall of music on my way out.

The end is the beginning. When I visited Santa Cruz more recently, the Choco children showed me yet another plant that they had learned was good for sickness. I reprised a short lesson on the radio in preparation for another upcoming workshop for teachers eager to integrate environmental and cultural heritage into their lessons. Three new babies had been born. This chapter synthesizes the findings from my study, presented in the preceding chapters, and points them toward future research and applications. It situates my research, and the framework of "embodied ecological heritage," in the current studies that aim to draw connections between traditional ecological knowledge (TEK) and heritage, making a case for the inclusion of wellness in a consideration of how heritage is constructed and perpetuated in indigenous communities. It makes a case for the incorporation of the past being crucial to the lived experience of the future.

HERITAGE AS WELLNESS PRACTICE

As my early ethnographic experience in Santa Cruz began, my research questions driving my everyday interactions and practices took shape. Both informal and formal data collection was undertaken in hope of illuminating them from as many directions as I was able toward the end of obtaining holistic responses. Fieldwork is, inevitably, unpredictable and certain perspectives are invariably more brightly lit than others. The answers together, however, are able to build a balanced picture of how wellness, heritage, and TEK/practice come together in the Mopan Maya community of Santa Cruz, providing a compelling case for the utility of the "embodied ecological heritage" framework in a consideration of Maya wellness in Santa Cruz.

Wellness and Ecological Experience

I began this study with a need and desire to determine how health and wellness were conceived by community members, and if, and in what ways, they were related to ecological practice and experience. In chapter 3, I detail how health and wellness are related, through their terminology, to strength and beauty. In this discussion, I demonstrate links between personal health and the health and beauty of the food; corn and chickens as examples. Health and wellness, defined broadly and used in tandem as a rejection of a mind/body dualism, are conceived of as

relating closely to both food consumed and work practices. The free listing, pile sorting, and subsequent multi-dimensional scaling analysis
pointed to a clear link between working together, a traditional ecological
practice of working the land, and health. Health was also linked with
traditional foods, particularly those collected and harvested in the high
bush. The planting and collection of these foods is easily described as
"ecological practice and experience." The data presented in chapter 4 also
speak to this connection, highlighting how illness and wellness are considered more crucial when they interfere with the ability to work. Working, again, is ecological practice, an ecological experience that is crucial to
the way a healthy life is conceived. The ethnographic examples presented
related to work show that it is essential to the conception of health.

The worry about the loss of connection to the land is exemplified in
chapters 5 and 6, through the discussion of education and the changes it
has brought, coupled with those that may occur through development,
the road paving as an example. The formal interview responses discussed
here demonstrate how the fear of these changes is present in Santa Cruz.
Wellness is linked to this worry and the worry is linked to changes in the
ecological practices. Wellness, in Santa Cruz, has been shown through the
data presented here to be linked clearly with environmental practice. It is
conceived of as the ability to work the land, the need to farm in a traditional way and the consumption of natural foods from the bush.

Heritage and Ecological Practice

Illuminating the place of heritage in the wellness/ecological practice
relationship necessitates understanding how environmental heritage is
conceived of and manifested in an individual and in a community. I
wondered if the heritage concept was related to environmental knowledge and skill or wellness—or if it was even salient at all.

"You think a lot!" This was a criticism leveled at me during my last
month in Santa Cruz. Maybe I wanted too hard to make sure I understood the connections I had come there to study, or maybe I just wanted
my leaving party to be perfect and kept changing my mind about what
we would eat. In my defense, how could I serve white chicken? I considered this in my field notes: "articulating the 'what-ifs' and trying to talk
about these abstract feelings of what they might change . . . are all pretty
counter to how folks live here—their pragmatism and the embodied nature of their knowledge. Life simply is—there aren't too many abstrac-
tions or complex what-if changes—adaptation just occurs—there is not a
big, overthinking 'I am adapting' moment. I am commented on for thinking too much because there is action here rather than intensive contem-
plation."

I offer this excerpt as a partial answer to the question of whether
environmental heritage is a salient concept in Santa Cruz. It is, for certain,

but it would never be discussed as such. The pragmatics of living in close connection to the natural environment do not lead to the conscious construction of a heritage concept. The manifestation of this heritage, however, is evident. The question of what makes everyday life, or the embodiment of ecological practices, "heritage" is nebulous, however, the ethnographic examples and discussion given throughout this study have sought to make this more concrete. The heritage "concept" in the sense that it is discussed across scholarly disciplines does have a degree of saliency in Santa Cruz. Much of this is derived from the conscious connection of "Maya traditions" to economic livelihoods in the wake of recent land rights case, discussed in chapter 2 and illuminated further in the following section. This noted, care should be taken not to over-emphasize the development and presence of distinct heritage concepts in Santa Cruz. I think doing so would be overlooking the way heritage is actually developed concurrently through both practice and consideration.

In chapter 6, I discuss the example of making sugar from cane as a potent illustration of how knowledge and skill diverge and how heritage conceptions can grow out of this diversion. Community members, in the face of the reality that sugar was unavailable in the shop, discussed the value of knowing how to make it, elevating it to an important heritage practice that was discussed as what "Maya people" could do. The skill, in this case, was directly linked to the elevation to heritage status. Indeed, chapters 4, 5, and 6 demonstrate how skill is connected to both learning and the acquisition of knowledge and how those skills, particularly as they relate to farming, are elevated to heritage status through their discussion as what "Maya people do." Chapter 4 describes how using these skills in work practice is crucial. "Doing" is a crucial component of "knowing" in terms of work. Learning to work in a particular way is an explicit expression of heritage and, conversely, rejecting what is thought of as traditional work might be seen as rejecting your heritage. Chapter 6 presents data that connects these ideas explicitly with wellness, demonstrating that the ability to make sugar, along with heritage practices in general, can help explain some of the variance in a household's wellness score.

The wellness/skill/heritage connection is discussed further in chapter 7 in references to the formal interview responses to changes in the community practices. All respondents refer to skills, practices, and "use of knowledge" related to the environment and the norms of farming practice as being more sound in the past. Threats to the health of individuals and the environment because of current practices and critique of community members who deviate too far from the more acceptable norms, affecting community wellness, were expressed. These responses were peppered with references to "Maya people" and clear constructions of heritage practices related to past farmers and their prowess. This discussion serves to answer much of this question, speaking generally about wellness in terms of what is best for the community and the children, and lead to a more detailed investigation into the embodied nature of the skills that may become heritage.

Skill and the Body

Having made the connection between who they are and their wellness, the residents of Santa Cruz were able to illuminate how environmental knowledge and skill related to the way the body is conceptualized. Chapter 3, in its description of food as relating to both heritage and wellness, includes the references made by community members to "Indian bodies" throughout the early part of my fieldwork. Later, chapter 7 covers the importance of not being lazy. Together, these illustrate a relationship between the body and what it does in the environment. There are many other references to "taking care" of one's body by not bathing at the incorrect time and the importance of understanding how to keep yourself dry if you are hot and on the farm during a rainstorm. Maya bodies, in this community-initiated discourse, need certain things and these things, without exception, have a direct relationship with knowing and understanding what you should and should not do in reference to your environment. Chapter 4 relates environmental reasons for sickness, the most frequent being the one mentioned above about staying dry. Chapter 3 stresses the importance of the knowledge and skill related to what people should grow and find to eat to give the Maya body what in needs for strength and health. I would argue that the environmental knowledge and skill is not simply related to the way the body is conceptualized, they are instrumental in the conceptualization of the healthy body in Santa Cruz.

Chapter 7 provides a discussion of a statement with high consensus relating the body feeling good to sweating and working. Hard work has emerged through the data presented here as the connection between environmental practice and the body. A skilled body, one that can work hard, is a healthy body. Having learned environmental skills and embodied environmental practice, there is no room to doubt these connections. Bodies are defined through the work that they do, and that work is directly connected to the natural environment.

The strength of this study was its use of multiple data collection strategies to approach rather broad research questions in a holistic and systematic way. My desire to capture the lived experience of being Maya in Santa Cruz through detailed participation, observation, and description was crucial to the guiding phenomenological orientation. This was balanced through the inclusion of more structured data collections and analyses. There was considerable overlap in the findings. For example, the importance of traditional work practices, land use, and foods emerged across the analyses as having important links to wellness in the community. Some discontinuities emerged. For example, while religion factored significantly in many practices related to heritage ethnographically, it was less significant statistically (Baines, forthcoming). While the changes in traditional social activities and work practices associated with Christian, non-Catholic religions are often noted by community members, the data show that these traditional practices may not have been impacted as severely in actuality. Heritage discourse and practice seemed to have endured, to a certain extent, through religious change, providing a deeper insight into the importance of everyday work for heritage maintenance. This addresses the embodied focus of the research and might have been missed if only one data collection method had been used. As a whole, the multiple methodologies utilized were successful in providing answers to my research questions, which open the door for further research and more specific and structured questions, collections, and analyses.

My presentation of the data has sought to demonstrate and clarify sometimes subtle connections and observations that speak to the core of the research questions. For example, the inclusion of "phenomenological process loops" has sought to illustrate, albeit simplistically at times, how ecological factors are directly related to both wellness and heritage as defined by traditional practice. They are designed to draw attention to both the ubiquity and strength of these connections, while recognizing the complexities involved in their mutual construction. They are not intended to be all-inclusive or exclusive but rather to give examples of nonlinear pathways by which heritage is constructed and wellness is maintained, and how these are interrelated through environmental interaction. The research presented is not exhaustive but hopes to open avenues of understanding the connections involved when ecological heritage is embodied.

THEORY AND PRACTICE

Wellness and Ecology

Using embodied ecological heritage as a framework for understanding the linkages outlined in the answers to the research questions allows for an analysis in multiple tiers. Heritage is a malleable construction, relying on how individuals and the community define and conceptualize it. Thinking about it as a source of collective pride, a way of conceiving of what "Maya people" do, forms a baseline for understanding how it makes a contribution to wellness. Thinking about it as a way of maintaining practices that are based on the "tried and tested" historical ecology of the living in the landscape adds another dimension to its wellness contributions. Embodied ecological heritage, however, takes this a step further, thinking about heritage as having a direct connection to the body and its state of wellness. In the preceding chapter, I discuss how a young man describes the burning of incense as not *actually* producing results but not doing any harm. Similarly, my neighbors once gave me warm ginger tea, telling me to drink it only after I bathed. This directive, they said was "just our tradition" and did not necessarily "work" for keeping the body well. My argument here is that these traditions and practices actually *do* something. There is an effect on the body through heritage practice that is not simply symbolic or cognitive, it is phenomenological. It is real.

The experience of participating in what can be considered rituals, whether they are everyday practices—such as baking tortillas or walking to the farm—or more elaborate celebrations—such as the killing of a pig for a planting or a wedding—is an embodied experience. This embodiment promotes wellness, I argue, through actual changes in the body. These changes are measurable in a number of ways: for example, observation and stress-level measurement through cortisol or blood pressure levels. For the purposes of this study, focus was placed on a measure of a community-defined definition of a well person, the environmental heritage and wellness assessment (see Baines, forthcoming, for further details.

While making this distinction about the nature of the way the body responds to ecological stimuli during the lifecourse is not novel, it is still in its infancy. Embodied ecological heritage, I argue, is a unique contribution to this field. Scholars have linked health and wellness to embodied experiences (Dressler and Bindon 2000; Lende 2005), further linking these to cognition and consensus. Other researchers have added a TEK component to the discussion of wellness from this perspective (see Godoy et al. 2005). None, however, have considered the construction of heritage in the study of traditional knowledge and considered how heritage plays out in practice or how it is embodied as part of everyday experience. None have drawn the explicit connections to wellness, broadly defined to include both physical and mental components. This is what I have hoped to provide here. While pushing beyond physical health/mental well-being divides and understanding wellness holistically is cast as a goal in medical anthropological discussions (Good 1993), there is a deficit of conceptual and methodological ways in which to make this push. This study hopes to go some distance toward addressing this. Fortunately, the anthropological toolkit is rich. A phenomenological perspective, in my view, necessitates rigorous ethnography and it is through the ethnographic examples of sensory experience that I hope the mechanism by which ecological heritage becomes embodied is illuminated.

Traditional Ecological Knowledge and Heritage

Embodied ecological heritage makes a significant contribution to the discussion linking heritage and TEK and practice. While, in one sense, highlighting TEK as "heritage" reinforces problematic conceptions of it as "traditional" in a static or symbolic sense as discussed throughout this study, on the other hand, heritage constructions and conceptions become increasingly salient to indigenous communities in a number of intersecting ways. Defining and cataloging TEK, and publicly recognizing it as heritage, adds influence within the global language of conservation in the face of shifting ownership associated with development. Popular heritage conceptions are certainly linked to tradition or the traditional. Krech (2005) describes "tradition" as "a vexed concept, mutable, open to external influence, and at times invented anew in succeeding generations [such that] one cannot assume that such knowledge is static or universally commanded." The possibility of invention or new influence constituting part of heritage becomes increasingly contentious when discussions enter legal or economic realms. Defining the "whos" and "whats" of heritage can have powerful consequences for development projects. These are particularly important when the foci of these projects include land use and management, as they increasingly do in the Toledo District.

The contribution to this discussion of the heritage/TEK relationship is particularly relevant when considering Santa Cruz in its current temporal and spatial position relative to the rest of the district, the country, and the region. Its role as a leader in the movement for Maya land rights in Belize has led to a more explicit consideration of how the connection to the land and land practices can be explained as integral to heritage. Articulating these connections, however transparent they might be to community members and scholars, has been challenging in the face of particular criteria expected from political or legal discourse. These challenges continue as the completion of the paved highway provides an even greater incentive for defining and managing community lands as they become more attractive in the development economy.

Community members are certainly aware of clarifying the TEK/heritage connection, with the pressure to do so coming in several forms. First, because of Santa Cruz's close proximity to Guatemala, many of the community members have seen firsthand the results of Maya land disenfranchisement and the negative effects of the use of chemical fertilizers and focusing on cash cropping. The paving of the highway to Guatemala through Santa Cruz makes the fear of the village becoming "like Guatemala" even more salient. The stark contrast between land use in the neighboring countries, which share a common tradition of *milpa* agriculture, gives an urgency to this discussion. Current negotiations with a Guatemalan oil company desiring to drill for oil on community lands in the Toledo District add even more weight. Second, unlike Guatemala,

Belize is comprised of several major ethnic groups, all of which trace their ancestry back for many generations prior to independence. Understanding traditional Maya land tenure as heritage practice, integral to the social and economic livelihoods of communities, makes an important distinction between Maya communities and those comprised of other ethnic groups who also possess their own traditional environmental knowledge and land use practices. This point about the how the traditional Maya land tenure system is both distinct and central to life in communities forms a crucial foundation for how heritage has been discussed and developed by activists and others in Belize.

Heritage activism does not always explicitly address TEK as a focus of interest. Often termed "intangible heritage," environmental knowledge can occupy a peripheral and sometimes problematic role in heritage construction. Identifying the current threatening force that is the catalyst for the convergence of cultural and natural heritages as "development," Lowenthal (2005) illustrates ways in which, more recently, the conceptions of the two heritages have become conflated, most notably as part of UNESCO initiatives. He critiques this conflation with a focus on TEK, exploring ways in which nature becomes separate from "us" and more associated with the "other," which often translates into indigenous people. Following this argument, heritage constructions reinforce the separation of TEK systems into contained and inflexible bodies of knowledge that has been critiqued as part of the theory and methodologies described above. The difference when considering heritage, perhaps, is the degree to which the knowledge "owners" have an influence over what is promoted and identified as this body of "traditional" or "heritage" knowledge.

Heritage activism can trace its roots to early ethnoecological considerations. It is important to note that it is often explicit that "a critical aspect of alternative strategy development . . . [using TEK] is the formulation and implementation of equitable indigenous rights policies" (Posey et al. 1984). The more current saliency of heritage conceptions, it can be argued, builds on this early TEK/development intersection. The explicit economic component of many ethnobotanical studies reinforces the links between ecology and heritage. Heritage and capital also have close links. For many indigenous people, "economic concerns trump green issues" (Krech 2005). This view is explored in more depth in chapter 5 in the discussion of money needed for school and the chopping of more forested areas to provide room for cash crops to generate this income. It is this sentiment that might be seen as nudging definitions and ownership of traditional environmental knowledge into the realm of "heritage" as opposed to "environmentalism" in its intersection with development models and programming.

Heritage is important in rooting a kind of ambiguous and hybrid knowledge in place and, as such, is tied to the concepts of both economic and cultural capital (Graham 2002). The primary economic and cultural uses of heritage—for tourism and socio-political emblematic effect respectively—are clearly outlined and more esoteric and "internal" factors related to heritage value are explored. This shift in focus away from TEK toward modern development models and then back again as the TEK is expressed as heritage is exemplified in the following ethnographic observation. "Those who are closest to the land and understand it the best are usually the poorest and have the least formal education. They are admired, on the one hand, for their knowledge of the land, and on the other hand, looked down upon for their old-fashioned ways" (Joyal 1996: 461). Anderson (2012) makes the more basic connection between TEK and heritage in his eloquent discussion of the continuity of the use of the maize plant among the Maya, stating, "it is a symbol of Mayaness, humanness, and equality—the antithesis of a symbol of unequal power."

In his chapter focused on the integration of TEK into management approaches, Merculieff et al. (2002) uses language that recognizes the political context surrounding TEK. More than simply an alternative system to be discovered, using TEK when designing management strategies supports a "marginalized way of knowing" (Merculieff et al. 2002: 523). The marginalization referenced here points to the effects of colonial expansion and its residual effects. While the act of perpetuating traditional knowledge may be more pragmatic and/or ritual in its practice, the politicized context of its use should not be overlooked (Anderson 2012). It is an easy observation that indigenous communities with traditional subsistence economies have been the subjects of various forms of colonization" (Langton and Rhea 2005). Particularly when considered within the frame of heritage ownership, celebration, and assertion, the colonization process and its subsequent political ramifications are quite salient in TEK discussions.

Embodied ecological heritage contributes to this particular intersection by allowing for the incorporation of these external forces in the development of heritage in relation to TEK, and ecological practices more generally, but turning the focus to how these forces play out in individual lives and, more specifically, individual bodies. This linkage to an understanding of wellness, and the role of the lived experience of engaging with TEK and practice, is a novel contribution to understand heritage constructions. This is timely for Santa Cruz and, I hope, for other communities like it, which are considering these changes and concepts.

Considering wellness in light of these changes, the contribution I present here is a beginning rather than an end. I offer data and discussion toward the development of body of research from multiple scholars, which offers an alternative to fixed genetic explanations for the way our brains and behavior affect our health. Through this contribution, I present a call for a "cognitive phenomenology," which, through this lens, is not the oxymoron scholars once thought. Discovering and disseminat-

ing that these ways of thinking are not fixed and how biological principles guiding cognition flex with environmental and social interactions
(Leatherman et al. 1993; Dressler 1990) is crucial to address issues of how
indigenous, and other historically underrepresented, communities might
achieve and maintain wellness. Critical Medical Anthropology can add
the sociopolitical structural consideration to this discussion and form a
"biocultural synthesis" (Leatherman et al. 1993). Phenomenological considerations, as I have shown in this study are a necessary addition. A
cognitive phenomenology can, I propose, take us far in terms of understanding how the complexities of what people do, and what they think
about what they do, affects their bodies, and their overall wellness.

While I recognize the abstraction, in one sense, of considering the
body as the seat of ecological heritage, it is making this connection that
finds utility in the application of the findings presented here. If heritage
is simply an idea, without a bodily connection, it would be easy to separate this idea from the people holding it. If heritage conceptions are developed through direct practice and interaction with the environment, as I
argue they are, they are much more crucial to the health and well-being
of individuals and communities. Following this, work to preserve heritage, or development and conservation work to change heritage practices, could benefit from understanding the complexities of the interaction. Embodied ecological heritage is a way, perhaps, for those involved
in this work to be more holistic.

Phenomenological research changes the researcher. This study has
changed me, deepening my understanding of how heritage can be constructed and changes beyond an abstraction. I have felt it in my body.
The Mopan Maya community of Santa Cruz is not remote or untouched
as it might be considered by others in the rest of the world, or even the
rest of Belize. The people who make their homes there do not exist in
isolation. Their heritage is consistently evolving. They use traditional ecological practices and pass on their TEK because it works. They are able to
maintain autonomy amid change. Their children learn how to keep themselves well in all respects: happy, healthy, prosperous. Negotiating
change is not easy for any community, but the residents of Santa Cruz do
it skillfully and with a consciousness of identity. Perhaps the way their
ecological heritage is embodied allows them this flexibility: it is not easily
cast off. Separation from the land is, in this sense, a more difficult process. It is my hope that my lived experience of Santa Cruz, reported here,
will reinforce the importance of these land/heritage/wellness connections
through equal parts systematic explanation and conscious celebration.

References

Adelson, N. 2009. "The Shifting Landscape of Cree Well-Being." In *Pursuits of Happiness: Well-Being in Anthropological Perspective*. Mathews and Izquierdo, eds. Berghahn Books

Anderson, E. N. 2012. "Yucatec Maya Botany and the 'Nature' of Science." *Journal of Ecological Anthropology* 14: 67–73.

Anderson, E. N., A. Dzib Zihum de Cen, F. Medina Tzuc, and P. Valdez Chale. 2005. *Political Ecology in a Yucatec Maya Community*. Illustrated edition. University of Arizona Press.

Baer, H. A. 1996. "Toward a Political Ecology of Health in Medical Anthropology." *Medical Anthropology Quarterly* 10(4): 451–54.

Baer, H. A., M. Singer, and I. Susser. 2003. *Medical Anthropology and the World System*. Greenwood Publishing Group.

Baines, K. 2008. "Substance and Strength: Rethinking Humoral Medical Conceptions among Indigenous Guatemalans." University of Oxford: MSc Thesis.

———. 2011. "Loops of Knowledge Shared: Embodied Ecological Heritage in Southern Belize." In *Sharing Cultures*. Porto, Portugal: Green Lines Institute for Sustainable Development, 301–9.

———. Forthcoming. "The Environmental Heritage and Wellness Assessment: Applying Quantitative Techniques to Traditional Ecological Knowledge and Wellness Relationships." *Journal of Ecological Anthropology*.

Baines, K. and R. K. Zarger. 2012. "Circles of Value: Integrating Maya Environmental Knowledge into Belizean Schools." In *The Anthropology of Environmental Education*. H. Kopnina, ed. Nova Science Publishers.

Berlin, B., D. E Breedlove, and P. H. Raven. 1973. "General Principles of Classification and Nomenclature in Folk Biology." *American Anthropologist* 75(1): 214–42.

Bernard, H. R. 2011. *Research Methods in Anthropology*. 5th Edition. AltaMira Press.

Binford, E. 2007 "Dynamics of Land Use among Maya of Southern Belize." University of Florida Masters Thesis.

Blake, J. 2002. "Developing a New Standard-Setting Instrument for the Safeguarding of Intangible Cultural Heritage: Elements for Consideration." UNESCO.

Borgatti, S. P. 1996. *ANTHROPAC 4.0*. Natick, MA: Analytic Technologies.

Borgerhoff Mulder, M., T. M. Caro, J. S. Chrisholm, J. P. Dumont, R. L. Hall, R. A. Hinde, and R. Ohtsuka. 1985. "The Use of Quantitative Observational Techniques in Anthropology [and Comments and Replies]." *Current Anthropology* 26(3): 323–35.

Bourbonnas-Spear, N., R. Awad, P. Maquin, V. Cal, P. Sanchez Vindas, L. Poveda, and J. T. Arnason. 2005. "Plant Use by the Q'eqchi'maya of Belize in Ethnopsychiatry and Neurological Pathology." *Economic Botany* 59(4): 326–36.

Bourdieu, P. 1977. *Outline of a Theory of Practice*. Cambridge University Press.

Brown, T., S. McLafferty, and G. Moon. 2009. *A Companion to Health and Medical Geography*. John Wiley and Sons.

Campbell, M. S., and S. J. Anaya. 2008. "The Case of the Maya Villages of Belize: Reversing the Trend of Government Neglect to Secure Indigenous Land Rights." *Human Rights Law Review* 8(2): 377–99.

Carman, J. 2003. *Archaeology and Heritage: An Introduction*. Continuum International Publishing Group.

Chambers, E. 2006. "Heritage Matters: Heritage, Culture, History, and Chesapeake Bay." Maryland Sea Grant College University of Maryland.

Chan, S. C. 2005. "Temple-Building and Heritage in China." *Ethnology* 44(1): 65–79.

Classen, C. 1990. "Sweet Colors, Fragrant Songs: Sensory Models of the Andes and the Amazon." *American Ethnologist* 17(4): 722–35.

Cliggett, L. and C. A. Pool. 2008. *Economies and the Transformation of Landscape*. Altamira.

Colby, B. N. 1987. "Well-Being: A Theoretical Program." *American Anthropologist* 89(4): 879–95.

Cooper, E. 2009. "Hunger of the Body, Hunger of the Mind: The Experience of Food Insecurity in Rural, Non-peninsular Malaysia." Graduate School Theses and Dissertations. http://scholarcommons.usf.edu/etd/1908.

Crooks, D. L. 1997. "Biocultural Factors in School Achievement for Mopan Children in Belize." *American Anthropologist* 99(3): 586–601.

Crossley, N. 1996. "Body-Subject/Body-Power: Agency, Inscription and Control in Foucault and Merleau-Ponty." *Body & Society* 2(2): 99–116.

Csordas, T. J. 1994. *Embodiment and Experience: The Existential Ground of Culture and Self*. Cambridge University Press.

Culleton, B. 2012. "Human Ecology, Agricultural Intensification and Landscape Transformation at the Ancient Maya Polity of Uxbenka, Southern Belize." Doctoral Dissertation. University of Oregon, Eugene.

D'Andrade, R. G. 1995. *The Development of Cognitive Anthropology*. Cambridge University Press.

Danziger, E. 1996. "Parts and Their Counterparts: Spatial and Social Relationships in Mopan Maya." *Journal of the Royal Anthropological Institute* 2(1): 67–82.

Diamond, J. 2011. *Collapse: How Societies Choose to Fail or Succeed: Revised Edition*. Revised. Penguin Books.

Dressler, W. W. 1990. "Lifestyle, Stress, and Blood Pressure in a Southern Black Community." *Psychosomatic Medicine* 52(2): 182–98.

Dressler, W. W., M. C. Balieiro, R. P. Ribeiro, and J. E. dos Santos. 2007. "A Prospective Study of Cultural Consonance and Depressive Symptoms in Urban Brazil." *Social Science & Medicine* 65(10): 2058–69.

Dressler, W. W., and J. R. Bindon. 2000. "The Health Consequences of Cultural Consonance: Cultural Dimensions of Lifestyle, Social Support, and Arterial Blood Pressure in an African American Community." *American Anthropologist* 102(2): 244–60.

Dunham, P. S., M. A. Abramiuk, L. S. Cummings, C. Yost, and T. J. Pesek. 2009. "Ancient Maya Cultivation in the Southern Maya Mountains of Belize: Complex and Sustainable Strategies Uncovered." *Antiquity* 83(319).

Dunning, N., and T. Beach. 2000. "Stability and Instability in Pre-Hispanic Maya Landscapes." *Imperfect Balance: Landscape Transformations in the Precolumbian Americas*, 179–202.

Dunning, N., T. Beach, P. Farrell, and S. Luzzadder-Beach. 1998. "Pre-Hispanic Agrosystems and Adaptive Regions in the Maya Lowlands." *Culture & Agriculture* 20(2–3): 87–101.

Emch, M. 2003. "The Human Ecology of Mayan Cacao Farming in Belize." *Human Ecology* 31(1): 111–31.

Emery K. F. 2007. "Assessing the Impact of Ancient Maya Animal Use." *Journal for Nature Conservation* 15(3): 184–95.

Escobar, A. 1996. "Construction Nature: Elements for a Post-Structuralist Political Ecology." *Futures* 28(4): 325–43.

Faust, B. B. 2001. "Maya Environmental Successes and Failures in the Yucatan Peninsula." *Environmental Science & Policy* 4(4–5): 153–69.

Fedick, S. L. 1996. "An Interpretive Kaleidoscope: Alternative Perspectives on Ancient Agricultural Landscapes of the Maya Lowlands." In *The Managed Mosaic: Ancient Maya Agriculture and Resource Use*, 107–31. Salt Lake City: University of Utah Press.

Fedick, S. L., and B. A. Morrison. 2004. "Ancient Use and Manipulation of Landscape in the Yalahau Region of the Northern Maya Lowlands." *Agriculture and Human Values* 21(2): 207–19.

Ford, J., and D. Martinez. 2000. "Traditional Ecological Knowledge, Ecosystem Science, and Environmental Management." *Ecological Applications* 10(5): 1249–50.

Foucault, M. 1973. *The Birth of the Clinic.* Psychology Press.

Gaskins, S. 2003. "From Corn to Cash: Change and Continuity within Mayan Families." *Ethos* 31(2): 248–73.

Van Gennep, A. 2004. *The Rites of Passage,* vol. 44. Routledge. http://books.google.com/books?hl=en&lr=&id=kJpkBH7mB7oC&oi=fnd&pg=PR7&dq=van+gennep+ritual&ots=xU1NeekVwF&sig=erEXLFatsiUOTo5Iei4Dxs1gZKU, accessed October 11, 2012.

Godoy, R., V. Reyes-García, E. Byron, W. R. Leonard, and V. Vadez. 2005. "The Effect of Market Economies on the Well-Being of Indigenous Peoples and on Their Use of Renewable Natural Resources." *Annual Review of Anthropology* 34(1): 121–38.

Goldin, L. R. 1994. "Household Ecology: Economic Change and Domestic Life among the Kekchi Maya of Belize." *Latin American Anthropology Review* 6(1): 56–57.

Good, B. J. 1993. *Medicine, Rationality and Experience: An Anthropological Perspective, 1990.* Cambridge University Press. http://books.google.com/books?hl=en&lr=&id=p7-Enmqb604C&oi=fnd&pg=PR8&dq=good+medicine+rationality&ots=1DXWSH9UBg&sig=aeJJqriAAL5W-tToMe54XTpWvq0, accessed October 11, 2012.

Graham, B. 2002. "Heritage as Knowledge: Capital or Culture?" *Urban Studies* 39(5–6): 1003–17.

Grandia, L. 2007a. Affidavit to the Belizean High Court. http://www.law.arizona.edu/depts/iplp/international/mayaBelize.cfm.

———. 2007b. *Unsettling: Land Dispossession and Enduring Inequity for the Q'eqchi'Maya in the Guatemalan and Belizean Frontier Colonization Process.* University of California, Berkeley.

Guest, G. 2002. "Market Integration and the Distribution of Ecological Knowledge within an Ecuadorian Fishing Community." *Journal of Ecological Anthropology* 6(1): 38–49.

Haines, S. 2012. "Meaningful Resources and Resource-full Meanings: Spatial and Political Imaginaries in Southern Belize." M. Janowski and T. Ingold, eds. In *Imagining Landscapes: Past, Present and Future,* 97–120. Farnham Ashgate Press.

Hammond, N. 1975. *Lubaantun, a Classic Maya Realm.* Harvard University Press

Heil, D. 2009. "Embodied Selves and Social Selves: Aboriginal Well-Being in Rural New South Wales, Australia." Mathews and Izquierdo. eds. In *Pursuits of Happiness: Well-Being in Anthropological Perspective,* 88–108. Berghahn Books.

Holmes, S. 2013. *Fresh Fruit, Broken Bodies: Migrant Farmworkers in the United States.* University of California Press.

Howard, P. 2003. *Heritage: Management, Interpretation, Identity.* Continuum International Publishing Group.

Hsu, E. 2007. "The Biocultural in the Cultural: The Five Agents and the Body Ecologic in Chinese Medicine." David Parkin and Stanley J. Ulijaszek, eds. In *Holistic Anthropology: Emergence and Convergence,* 91–126. Berghahn Books.

Hunn, E. 1982. "The Utilitarian Factor in Folk Biological Classification." *American Anthropologist* 84(4): 830–47.

Ingold, T. 2000. *The Perception of the Environment: Essays on Livelihood, Dwelling and Skill.* Psychology Press.

Izquierdo, C. 2005. "When 'Health' Is Not Enough: Societal, Individual and Biomedical Assessments of Well-Being among the Matsigenka of the Peruvian Amazon." *Social Science & Medicine* 61(4): 767–83.

Johns, T. 1999. *Plant Constituents and the Nutrition and Health of Indigenous Peoples. Ethnoecology*/*Situated Knowledge, Located Lives.* University of Arizona Press.

Johnson, A., and R. Sackett. 1998. "Direct Systematic Observation of Behavior." *Handbook of Methods in Cultural Anthropology:* 301–31.

Joyal, E. 1996. "The Palm Has Its Time: An Ethnoecology of Sabal Uresana in Sonora, Mexico." *Economic Botany* 50(4): 446–62.

Kapferer, B. 1988. "Gramsci's Body and a Critical Medical Anthropology." *Medical Anthropology Quarterly* 2(4): 426–32.

Kearns, R. A., and W. M. Gesler. 1998. *Putting Health into Place: Landscape, Identity, and Well-Being.* Syracuse University Press.

Keller, G., W. Stinnesbeck, T. Adatte, B. Holland, D. Stüben, M. Harting, C. de Leon, and J. de la Cruz. 2003. "Spherule Deposits in Cretaceous–Tertiary Boundary Sediments in Belize and Guatemala." *Journal of the Geologic Society, London* 160: 783–95.

Kennett, D. J., S. F. Breitenbach, V. V. Aquino, Y. Asmerom, J. Awe, J. U. Baldini, P. Bartlein, B. J. Culleton, C. Ebert, C. Jazwa, M. J. Marci, N. Marwan, V. Polyak, K. M. Prufer, H. E. Ridley, H. Sodemann, B. Winterhalder, and G. H. Haug. 2012. "Development and Disintegration of Maya Political Systems in Response to Climate Change." *Science* 338(6108), 788–91.

Kirsch, S. 2007. "Indigenous Movements and the Risks of Counterglobalization: Tracking the Campaign against Papua New Guinea's Ok Tedi Mine." *American Ethnologist* 34(2): 303–21.

Krech III, S. 2005. "Reflections on Conservation, Sustainability, and Environmentalism in Indigenous North America." *American Anthropologist* 107(1): 78–86.

Lampman, A. 2012. "How Folk Classification Interacts with Ethnoecological Knowledge: A Case Study from Chiapas, Mexico." *Journal of Ecological Anthropology* 14: 39–51.

Langton, M., and Z. M. Rhea. 2005. "Traditional Indigenous Biodiversity-Related Knowledge." *Australian Academic and Research Libraries* 36(2): 47(26).

Lauer, M., and S. Aswani. 2009. "Indigenous Ecological Knowledge as Situated Practices: Understanding Fishers' Knowledge in the Western Solomon Islands." *American Anthropologist* 111(3): 317–29.

Leatherman, T. L., and A. Goodman. 2005. "Coca-Colonization of Diets in the Yucatan." *Social Science & Medicine* 61(4): 833–46.

Leatherman, T. L., A. H. Goodman, and R. B. Thomas. 1993. "On Seeking Common Ground between Medical Ecology and Critical Medical Anthropology." *Medical Anthropology Quarterly* 7(2). New Series: 202–7.

Lende, D. H. 2005. "Wanting and Drug Use: A Biocultural Approach to the Analysis of Addiction." *Ethos* 33(1): 100–24.

Levin, B. W., and C. H. Browner. 2005. "The Social Production of Health: Critical Contributions from Evolutionary, Biological, and Cultural Anthropology." *Social Science & Medicine* 61(4): 745–50.

Lowenthal, D. 2005. "Natural and Cultural Heritage." *International Journal of Heritage Studies* 11(1): 81–92.

Mark, G. T., and A. C. Lyons. 2010. "Maori Healers' Views on Wellbeing: The Importance of Mind, Body, Spirit, Family and Land." *Social Science & Medicine* (1982) 70(11): 1756–64.

Mathews, G., and C. Izquierdo. 2009. "Anthropology, Happiness, and Well-Being." In *Pursuits of Happiness: Well-Being in Anthropological Perspective.* Mathews and Izquierdo, eds. Berghahn Books, 1–22.

Mathews, H. F. 1983. "Context-Specific Variation in Humoral Classification." *American Anthropologist* 85(4): 826–47.

McDade, T. W. 2002. "Status Incongruity in Samoan Youth: A Biocultural Analysis of Culture Change, Stress, and Immune Function." *Medical Anthropology Quarterly* 16(2): 123–50.

McGregor, D. 2005. "Coming Full Circle: Indigenous Knowledge, Environment, and Our Future." *American Indian Quarterly* 28(3): 385–410.

McKercher, B., and H. D. Cros. 2002. *Cultural Tourism: The Partnership between Tourism and Cultural Heritage Management.* Haworth Hospitality Press.

McMullin, J. 2009. *The Healthy Ancestor: Embodied Inequality and the Revitalization of Native Hawai'ian Health,* vol. 2. Left Coast Press.

Medina, L. K. 1998. "History, Culture, and Place-Making: 'Native' Status and Maya Identity in Belize." *Journal of Latin American Anthropology* 4(1): 134–65.

————. 2003. "Commoditizing Culture: Tourism and Maya Identity." *Annals of Tourism Research* 30(2): 353–68.

Meggers, B. J. 1954. "Environmental Limitation on the Development of Culture." *American Anthropologist* 56(5): 801–24.

Merculieff, L., J. R. Stepp, F. S. Wyndham, and R. K. Zarger. 2002. "Linking Traditional Knowledge and Wisdom to Ecosystem Based Approaches in Research and Management: Supporting a Marginalized Way of Knowing." In *Ethnobiology and Biocultural Diversity: Proceedings of the 7th International Congress of Ethnobiology, Athens, Georgia, USA, October 2000,* 523–31.

Merleau-Ponty, M. 2002. *Phenomenology of Perception.* Psychology Press.

Messer, E. 1987. "The Hot and Cold in Mesoamerican Indigenous and Hispanicized Thought." *Social Science & Medicine* 25(4): 339–46.

Miller, T. 2011. *Maize as Material Culture? Amazonian Theories of Persons and Things.*

Morehart, C. T., and C. G. B. Helmke. 2008. "Situating Power and Locating Knowledge: A Paleoethnobotanical Perspective on Late Classic Maya Gender and Social Relations." *Archeological Papers of the American Anthropological Association* 18(1): 60–75.

Morris, B. 1984. "Macrofungi of Malawi: Some Ethnobotanical Notes." *Bulletin of the British Mycological Society* 18(1): 48–57.

Nazarea, V. D. 1999. *Ethnoecology: Situated Knowledge/Located Lives.* University of Arizona Press.

Olwig, K. F. 1999. "The Burden of Heritage: Claiming a Place for a West Indian Culture." *American Ethnologist* 26(2): 370–88.

Parkin, D. 2007. "Wafting on the Wind: Smell and the Cycle of Spirit and Matter." *Journal of the Royal Anthropological Institute* 13(s1): S39–S53.

Parks, S. 2009. *Archaeological Ethics and the Struggle for Community Legitimacy in the Maya Archaeoscape.* ProQuest.

————. 2010. "The Collision of Heritage and Economy at Uxbenka, Belize." *International Journal of Heritage Studies* 16(6): 434–48.

Posey, D. A, J. Frechione, J. Eddins, L. Da Silva, D. Myers, D. Case, and P. Macbeath. 1984. "Ethnoecology as Applied Anthropology in Amazonian Development." *Human Organization* 43(2): 95–107.

Prufer, K. M., H. Moyes, B. Culleton, A. Kindon, and D. Kennett. 2011. "Formation of a Complex Polity on the Eastern Periphery of the Maya Lowlands." *Latin American Antiquity* 22(2): 199–223.

Prufer, K. M., A. E. Thompson, and D. J. Kennett. 2015. "Evaluating airborne LiDAR for detecting settlements and modified landscapes in disturbed tropical environments at Uxbenka, Belize." *Journal of Archaeological Science* 57: 1–13.

Purcell, T. W. 1998. "Indigenous Knowledge and Applied Anthropology: Questions of Definition and Direction." *Human Organization* 57(3): 258–72.

Pyburn, K. A. 1996. "The Political Economy of Ancient Maya Land Use: The Road to Ruin." In *The Managed Mosaic: Ancient Maya Agriculture and Resource Use,* 236–50. Salt Lake City: University of Utah Press.

————. 1998. "Smallholders in the Maya Lowlands: Homage to a Garden Variety Ethnographer." *Human Ecology* 26(2): 267–86.

Quinlan, M. B., and R. J. Quinlan. 2007. "Modernization and Medicinal Plant Knowledge in a Caribbean Horticultural Village." *Medical Anthropology Quarterly* 21(2): 169–92.

Randall, R. A. 1987. "The Nature of Highly Inclusive Folk-botanical Categories." *American Anthropologist* 89(1): 143–46.

Randall, R. A., and E. S. Hunn. 1984. "Do Life-forms Evolve or Do Uses for Life? Some Doubts about Brown's Universals Hypotheses." *American Ethnologist* 11(2): 329–49.

Reyes-García, V., E. Kightley, I. Ruiz-Mallén, et al. 2010. "Schooling and Local Environmental Knowledge: Do They Complement or Substitute Each Other?" *International Journal of Educational Development* 30(3): 305–13.

Ridley, H. E., Asmerom, Y., Baldini, J. U. L., Breitenbach, S. F. M., Aquino, V. V., Prufer, K. M., Brendan J. Culleton, B. J., Polyak, V., Lechleitner, F. A., Kennett, D. J., Zhang, M., Marwan, N., Macpherson, C. G, Baldini, L. M., Xiao, T., Peterkin, J. L., Awe, J., Haug, G. H. 2015. "Aerosol Forcing of the Position of the Intertropical Convergence Zone since AD 1550." *Nature Geoscience* 8: 195–200.

Robbins, P., N. Jan, S. Moore, A. J. Secor, and J. Wainwright. 2010. "Reading Joel Wainwright's Decolonizing Development: Colonial Power and the Maya." *Political Geography*.

Scarborough, V. L. 2003. "How to Interpret an Ancient Landscape." *Proceedings of the National Academy of Sciences of the United States of America* 100(8): 4366–68.

Singer, M. 1993. "A Rejoinder to Wiley's Critique of Critical Medical Anthropology." *Medical Anthropology Quarterly* 7(2). New Series: 185–91.

Steinberg. 2002. "The Globalization of a Ceremonial Tree: The Case of Cacao (Theobroma Cacao) among the Mopan Maya." *Economic Botany* 56(1): 58–65.

Tedlock, B. 1987. "An Interpretive Solution to the Problem of Humoral Medicine in Latin America." *Social Science & Medicine* 24(12): 1069–83.

Thompson, J. E. 1930. *Ethnology of the Mayas of Southern and Central British Honduras.* Chicago: Field Museum Press.

Thompson, A. E., and K. M. Prufer. 2015. "Settlement Distributions and Social Organization at Ix Kuku'il and Uxbenka, Toledo District, Belize." Presentation at the Belize Archaeology and Anthropology Symposium, San Ignacio, Belize. 2 July 2015.

Toledo Alcaldes Association and Toledo Maya Cultural Council. 1997. *Maya Atlas: The Struggle to Preserve Maya Land in Southern Belize.* North Atlantic Books.

Vermonden, D. 2009. "Reproduction and Development of Expertise within Communities of Practice." In *Landscape, Process and Power: A Re-evaluating Traditional Environmental Knowledge,* 205–29. Berghahan Books.

Wainwright, J. 2007. Affidavit to the Belizean High Court. http://www.law.arizona.edu/depts/iplp/international/mayaBelize.cfm.

———. 2008. *Decolonizing Development: Colonial Power and the Maya.* Wiley-Blackwell.

Wainwright, J., and J. Bryan. 2009. "Cartography, Territory, Property: Postcolonial Reflections on Indigenous Counter-mapping in Nicaragua and Belize." *Cultural Geographies* 16(2): 153–78.

Wiley, A. S. 1992. "Adaptation and the Biocultural Paradigm in Medical Anthropology: A Critical Review." *Medical Anthropology Quarterly* 6(3). New Series: 216–36.

Wilk, R. R. 1985. "The Ancient Maya and the Political Present." *Journal of Anthropological Research* 41(3): 307–26.

———. 1991. "Household Ecology: Economic Change and Domestic Life among the Kekchi Maya in Belize."

———. 2007. Affidavit to the Belizean High Court. http://www.law.arizona.edu/depts/iplp/international/mayaBelize.cfm.

Young, I. M. 1980. "Throwing Like a Girl: A Phenomenology of Feminine Body Comportment Motility and Spatiality." *Human Studies* 3(1): 137–56.

Zarger, R. K. 2002. *Children's Ethnoecological Knowledge: Situated Learning and the Cultural Transmission of Subsistence Knowledge and Skills among Q'eqchi'Maya.* University of Georgia.

———. 2009. "Mosaics of Maya Livelihoods: Readjusting to Global and Local Food Crises." *NAPA Bulletin* 32(1): 130–51.

———. 2011. "Learning Ethnobiology: Creating Knowledge and Skills about the Living World." In *Ethnobiology.* E. N. Anderson, D. Pearsall, E. Hunn, and N. Turner, eds. John Wiley & Sons, Inc.

Zarger, R. K., and J. R. Stepp. 2004. "Persistence of Botanical Knowledge among Tzeltal Maya Children." *Current Anthropology* 45(3): 413–18.

Zarger, Rebecca, S. Parks, and K. Prufer. 2008. "Learning the Past and Valuing the Present: Education Initiatives at Uxbenka." Belize Archaeology Symposium.

Index

About the Author

Kristina Baines is a social anthropologist on a mission to uncover ecological connections to health and happiness, working primarily with indigenous and immigrant communities in Belize and in the United States. She has collaboratively developed environmental and cultural heritage educational materials based on local research in the Toledo District, Belize (www.teacha.org), and hopes, through the use of technology, to promote the wide dissemination of anthropological ideas and their applications (www.coolanthropology.com). She holds a PhD in Applied Anthropology (University of South Florida, 2012), an MSc in Medical Anthropology (University of Oxford, 2008), an MA in Social Anthropology (Florida Atlantic University, 2001), and a BA in Anthropology with Environmental Studies (Florida Atlantic University, 1995). She is an assistant professor of anthropology and faculty for academic technology at Guttman Community College, the City University of New York in Manhattan.